BROADWAY PLAY PUBLISHING, INC.

ONE ACTS AND MONOLOGUES FOR WOMEN

by

Ludmilla Bollow

D1264585

249 WEST 29 STREET NEW YORK NY 10001 (212) 563-3820

ONE ACTS AND MONOLOGUES FOR WOMEN

Copyright 1983 by Ludmilla Bollow

First printing: July 1983

ISBN: 0-88145-008-1

Cover art by William Sloan/THREE.
Design by Marie Donovan.
Set in Baskerville by BakerSmith Type, NYC.
Printed and bound by BookCrafters, Inc., Chelsea MI.

THE WOMAN WITH 27 CHILDREN

Scene opens:

Bare Stage or platform.

Center Right, a worn wooden rocking chair. Faded loose knit shawl over arm.

Center Left, a hand-carved wooden chair, with a quilt of delicately muted designs draped over.

WOMAN enters slowly, wearing a long loose gown of homespun material, earthspun color.

She's an older woman, her age not easily determined. She carries a huge object, wrapped in a handwoven blanket.

Cautiously she goes to the window area, looking out front.

Peers into distance.

Nobody out there . . . Least I don't think so—

Maybe they won't come today . . . Maybe today isn't the day. The letter— I don't remember if it said today or not—Vernon, he would have remembered . . .

Come, we'll sit by the window for a little bit. There's time.

Sit in the chair your papa made for you. He never did get to finish it . . . Never finished you either.

Begins unwrapping blanket. A huge crudely carved wooden doll, resembling a grown person is revealed. It is not finished, so the gender is not apparent. Arms and legs are flexible. It is dressed in a long gold night robe. The eyes, which move, seem alive, imparting a mystical quality to this strange replica of a human being.

WOMAN *sets figure in rocking chair.*

There, now you can watch the birdies. You missed them, didn't you. We haven't watched them for such a long time. And I haven't fed them since—

After, when we're sure no one's coming, I'll put you in the wagon, and take you for a little trip in the field, look for chaff and seeds—

Yes. I know you don't like being locked up in that basement day after day. It's dark—damp—down there. I know . . . I hear you children crying all night.

But we're not going to cry today, are we. The sun is shining and—

I'm so glad papa finished your eyes . . .

He always worked so hard on the eyes . . . Days sometimes . . .

He was always seeking to capture—the soul of the piece, he said. "And I can never tell if it's there, till I finish the eyes."

Was like he had X-ray vision. He could look at an ugly piece of stone—a plain block of wood—and see everything beautiful that lay within. And he had that power, that special gift to release everything beautiful that anything contained.

He could do that with people, too, you know.

He did it with me . . .

Released everything good and wonderful inside me.

Then he went away—it stopped coming out . . .

She sits in the chair, absently fingering the quilt. Mood shifts to happier remembering.

How many times I sat looking out this window. And you children, you'd all be out there sitting around the Magic Circle, on your carved wooden chairs, watching the birds swoop, butterflies dance—the flowers swaying in the sun.

And you'd be watching papa too. Just as I did. Going about his stonecutting, carving, chiseling—inside that Magic Circle. As if he were performing for an audience. Seems he needed—wanted you children there to watch him.

Way back, at the beginning, it was just me. But then, when the family got bigger—I had more housework to do. Still whenever I could, I'd sit by this window, do my sewing, sunlight bouncing on my materials.

Oh—and him—skin glistening in the sun. Leather apron and gloves doing their own dance. Chisel moving like splashing diamonds.

A bare piece of wood—a giant block of stone—His magic fingers would fly, and pretty soon, the form would begin taking shape—emerging as if in slow motion—a tree with flowers—a dancing bear—an ancient Indian . . .

And he'd line them all up across the back. Just like he had another audience in that background. Such a sight! Such a sight . . . .

All his creatures are gone now . . .

And so is he . . .

Pause. Rocks in chair.

You children are all I have left. And now they want to take you away too . . .

And they want to take this house . . . Where would we go . . . I don't know what to do. He never told me what to do.

Up to window area. Back to brighter remembering.

"Heaven on the Hill," that's the name he picked for this place.

"I want to build a special house, Angel, just for you and the children—among the trees and birds, away from everything else.

"Look, Angel, the wonderful site I found—on top of this hill.

We can look out over the whole world, and then look straight up into the heavens."

My real name was Angelina, but he always called me Angel—"his very own special Angel." And when he said it—"Angel," I always felt as if I could soar above the whole earth—as if wings were taking my heart away.

I haven't felt like that—

So, he built this house, piece by piece, log by log.

"Love goes into every chisel mark," he said—"You'll feel it, Angel, like special arms wrapped around you, in the cold of winter, the warmth of summer. The children will know it too."

The house stood, waiting.

The children never came—

We were married five years—and then I got this strange sickness. I still don't know what it was. Fever. Visions . . . Trembling . . .

And Vernon, always at my side. His hands holding mine so tightly, soothing my forehead, feeding me . . . Those special hands, that could turn stone into soft flowers, wood into bird feathers—they were the gentlest hands, love flowing from every finger.

And, in our private moments, his hands, sent electricity through every part of my body. I didn't know such feelings could exist in a human being . . .

I try to bring them back. But I can't—not without him . . .

When I was sick—my head spinning so I couldn't see—I could always feel his hands—like rays of light were passing through my body.

He's the only reason I lived through that time.

But I never wanted to outlive him . . . Never . . .

Sits and rocks a bit and fondles quilt.

I cried. Oh, I cried so when Vernon told me—he was crying too—that I could never have children.

We both wanted them so. But the doctor told him—

Everything changed then, once I knew—or maybe it was the sickness—I don't know—I just couldn't think right—tears falling all the time . . .

And Vernon, he couldn't stay with me all the time—he had to go to his job at the factory.

When we were first married and I couldn't bear to have him leave me, for even a minute—I'd say to him, clinging to him, just as he was getting ready to go out the door—

"Don't go to work today, Vernon, stay home with me, love. I can't bear for you to be away for so long . . ."

"A man has to do certain things," he'd say. "Even when I'm away from you, Angel, I'm always with you . . ." And he'd kiss me and leave, so quickly.

And I'd stand at the top of this hill, watching him walk down the winding pathway, getting smaller and smaller—and I'd feel so empty—and lost—till he came home again.

He'd leave at six in the morning. Get home after three. Such a tired look on his face. He greeted me first, then went straight to his statues, working till it got too dark to see.

"Sell some of those pieces you make," I'd say. "They are more beautiful than anything I've seen in any of the parks or museums. Then you wouldn't have to leave here every day, work in that other place."

"No. I can never sell my work," he'd answer. "They are pieces of myself—extensions of my inner being—I can't put a price on such things. I can't sell parts of myself . . ."

So, he would work in that chair factory every day, making chairs by machines. "Chairs without souls," he called them.

"I think about things there, Angel, while my machine automatically spindles a chair leg. I see visions in my head—about my next piece of wood, and what I'm going to create out of it. I don't even hear sometimes when anyone's talking to me. But, I do good work. I always do good work. I want to provide for you, and the children."

But there were no children . . .

Pause. Gets up and walks around. As if touching objects.

Every Christmas Vernon would make me something special.
A delicately carved rose pin—maybe, a new table—perhaps a
polished piece of glass to hang in my window. I never knew
beforehand. Each present was different. And they were all
made in love. Given in love. And somehow the love stayed
with them. Polished into them for a lifetime.

When I'd look at them, touch them *(fondles wooden carving on
a cord around her neck)* the love would still be there, glowing
like some inner light.

That year, after the sickness, I couldn't guess what would be
under the tree.

Me—I always made Vernon some article of clothing, maybe
a new warm flannel shirt, or a robe of rainbows, piecing
together leftover strips of cloth. He was hard on his work
clothes, wore them out pretty fast. Rough stone cutting them,
bare wood rubbing. So, I would make him practical clothes—
not anything fancy—or even pretty, like his presents to me.

He gave me so much beauty—I wanted to give him something
back. So, I started embroidering little flowers or butterflies
on his clothes. Teensy little roses on those heavy flannel shirts.

And he'd say, "Angel, you should make the flowers bigger,
so everyone can see them, enjoy their beauty . . . Put more
of them on—a whole border, if you have the time. They're
even better than live flowers, because you made them."

And he'd wear his embroidered shirts to the factory too. Didn't
matter what the men down there said. Never mattered at all
what others said, only what he thought of himself.

Those shirts wore out quick. Yet, somehow the pieces with
the embroidery would still be bright and beautiful. So I began
saving them, and started a nice quilt—just kept adding pieces
to it . . .

After he went, I couldn't, I just couldn't, embroider any more flowers . . .

Vernon valued anything hand made. Believed we left something of ourselves in everything we did.

Picks up shawl, drapes it over her, hugging it.

This shawl—they said my mother made it. I was wrapped in it when they brought me to the orphanage. She's been gone—how long now—but I still feel a special warmth when I wear it—as if parts of her were worked into it. Her fingers touched every bit of this yarn—

I never knew my mama—only through this shawl . . .

Drapes shawl around figure.

Here, you wear it for awhile. Will make you feel better.

Sits in rocker, rocking—back into memories.

Anyway, that Christmas, the one after I found out I couldn't ever have children—under the tree— Oh, it was always such a gorgeous tree. Vernon would cut it down himself. Carved ornaments. Made dazzling things from pine cones and berries—he could make anything into beauty.

He set the tree in the window, just at the right angle, so the moon would shine on it in a certain way.

That's how he faced the house, so the moon would shine through this window—and a special circle window in the ceiling . . .

At the stroke of twelve—we'd open our gifts to each other.

I'd always open mine first. I could never wait. Usually he could guess what he was getting anyway.

Neither of us got other presents. Both our families gone. His—killed in a fire— Mine—I never really knew.

I was raised in so many different homes—and even living with people, I always felt alone—till Vernon found me. I was doing kitchen work at the hospital. Vernon was delivering vegetables . . .

Anyway, this one Christmas, his present to me was wrapped in a soft new blanket. I was truly curious. Usually they were in a big box, even if it was only a tiny carved bird . . .

Oh, he'd sit by the kerosene lamp, winter nights, carving all those little things. And I'd read to him. I couldn't read too well at first. Couldn't even say the big words—had to spell them out. But Vernon, he was patient, helped me. He knew so many things. A brilliant man. I only went to second grade.

During summer—there wasn't time for reading. He'd work till dark and I'd have to call him in—make sure he heard me, he'd be so involved. And when he came in, the lines from the factory, they'd be erased from his face and he'd be glowing in a special way.

You ever seen pictures of saints, where a light shines around them. That's how he'd be, after doing his work . . .

Then after supper, we'd sit in the twilight, sometimes holding hands. Talking—or not talking. The clock ticking. Night birds calling.

"The sounds of the universe passing," he'd whisper.

Once a month, during the winter, he'd stop at the library, bring home books—all by the same author.

By the time we'd get through those books, we'd feel we knew that author pretty well. He or she became our special friend.

When Vernon would mention what Henry Longfellow said, I knew he wasn't talking about someone from his job—He always called the factory his job—his work was making his creations.

Anyway, we never owned books. Well, a bible, a dictionary—and a few that were gifts. But Vernon, he liked reading books someone else had read, like they left a little part of themselves inside the book. He liked the idea of a library—sharing ideas—knowledge.

He was always sorry he couldn't share his statues. Didn't even want people to know about them. Never did say exactly why, but I think maybe he was afraid they might destroy them—being out in the open like that.

He wanted them left there—to weather in the elements.

"They won't really be finished for years," he'd say. "I did my part—nature has to do the rests." Always believed in working with nature—using natural materials to begin with, and natural things, sun, rain, to finish them.

"Angel," he'd say, "after I'm gone—then they'll be shared. I'm willing them to the museum. All my life I've never sold anything—but when I'm no longer around to watch over them, I want them in a place where they will be protected—where everyone, rich and poor, can enjoy them."

He always thought I'd pass on before him—I don't know why, I guess, because of the sickness I had . . .

Puts figure down. Gets up. Paces.

So, that Christmas, our fifth together, there was this big blanket under the tree.

"Go on, open your present," he whispered. Oh, and he had such a smile, like never before.

I picked up the bundle. A warmth was coming through it, as if something living was inside. I held it carefully in my arms, folded back a bit—and there—there inside was this lovely baby's face—smiling back at me.

I couldn't believe it.

He had carved me a real live baby. Oh, and he had rubbed in the colors so it looked alive. Tiny arms—tiny legs—they moved. The eyes, gathered in all the light of the room. Opened and closed. That baby even cried . . .

"There's your child, Angel," he whispered. "If I can't give

you a child any other way—this one is made from my flesh
and blood also."

I cried. I cried so. Because, after all those years, that terrible
hungry longing inside me—that deep lonely feeling, that
Vernon mostly cured, but was still waiting for something
else—this baby, this beautifully hand carved child—born of
Vernon's hands, was now part of our family, joining us together even closer. A special gift of love.

New Year's day we christened her—Evangeline, in honor of
our friend Henry Longfellow. We made him her godfather.

That winter, Vernon carved a cradle, a high chair. And I
embroidered baby clothes. Oh, did I embroider baby clothes.

Evangeline sat at the table while we ate. Slept in our room.

And when Vernon came home, after kissing me—he'd kiss
Evangeline, then go to his work, whistling.

I'd sing lullabies, stored up, waiting to be sung—and rock her
in this chair. And I wasn't lonely anymore in the daytime
while Vernon was gone to his job.

Every year after that, under the tree, would be a brand new
child. Each one a little older looking than the one before.
Sometimes a boy, sometimes a girl. I'd never know beforehand. Yet somehow the genders always evened up.

But, you were never finished—so I could never tell—

Such beautiful children. Some fat. Some thin. Smiling.
Somber. But always, those same penetrating eyes.

"It's part of their inherited genes," Vernon would say, "their
family trait."

Christmas was the birthday for all of you. And New Year's
for the christening.

We'd pick the godfather or godmother author—line up all
their books and then choose a character's name for the
child . . .

Stroke of midnight, we'd make a toast, some special offering to each other for the year, with chokecherry wine—then christen the baby.

Sometimes we couldn't agree on a name, then Vernon would always say, "You choose, Angel, you're the one that has to be calling them."

I thought he might get tired—making a bigger child every year. Same christening party—

Yet, each year, the event seemed dearer. Neither of us had had childhood Christmases, none worth remembering—so we were building our own traditions. Storing up family remembrances.

Vernon did paintings of you children too—lovely portraits. Finished before each child was born, because Vernon knew exactly how you would turn out. No other parents can do that . . .

Each child had three sets of clothes, a night gown, every day wear and one special fancy outfit—for those special occasions—and prayer service we held each Sunday.

"You finish the cooking and baking," Vernon would say. "I'll dress the children."

He was so gentle with them. Talking to them as he put on their clothes. He remembered their names too. I couldn't always.

I wanted to paint their names on them. But Vernon said that wouldn't be right. Real children didn't have names painted on them. And they wouldn't mind if I mixed them up a bit.

Twenty seven. Twenty seven children he gave me . . .

Oh, at the end, his hands were crippled up so, with the arthritis—and the fine details weren't there anymore, but they appeared even more beautiful somehow.

He had perfected bringing out the human in a piece of wood—with only a few deft lines. He stopped painting them later too. Older children had only natural grains of polished wood.

"They're no special race, anyway," Vernon said. "You know, I think we've bred a new one . . .

Towards the end, his other output slowed down some.

Then, he was laid off from the factory—just couldn't keep up with the machines anymore. Gave him more time with his art works. But, he made fewer pieces. Still, each one was more exquisite than the last.

Legs were stiffening too. It got harder for him to get up and down the path, especially in winter.

I remember—the first time the library man came up. He was worried because Vernon didn't show up on the first of the month to pick out his supply of winter books.

Nobody ever came to visit us. Gate at bottom. Such a steep path to climb. Mailbox was at the bottom of the hill. Sometimes, in the later days, we didn't pick up our mail for weeks. Was never anything important anyways.

So, the library man came up, through the snow, with some books by a new author he thought Vernon would like.

I was watching Vernon through the window, showing that man his artpieces, brushing the snow off—the man was saying—"Beautiful! Breathtaking! I didn't know you were such an accomplished artist!"

Vernon opened the door, calling in, "Set an extra place at the table, Angel."

I didn't know what to do. We had never had anyone to supper before. Vernon knew I was shy around people. Skittish. I could talk to Vernon about anything, but—

With other people—I'd get all tight inside. Couldn't say a thing.

What about the children? They'd be frightened of a stranger too. Should I hide them? What would this man think of twenty three—yes, I think it was twenty three then—children around the table.

There wasn't even time to put on their good clothes.

I had a big pot of garden stew—each child had their own bowl, but we only put a spoonful up to their mouth. He'd know—he'd guess—

I'd just have to trust Vernon. I wouldn't say anything—let Vernon do all the talking.

Children circled the table. Usually they sat there most of the day. I'd take a different one outside each day—a ride in the wagon—walk in the woods.

They looked frightened when I said we were having a guest for dinner. But I told them "to behave, be on their best manners."

I could hear Vernon and the man's steps getting closer—

"You built this house yourself, Vernon?" he sounded real surprised.

"Oh yes," Vernon said, "faced it so we could view the world, yet no one could see us way up here—sheltered by the trees and the stars."

"I had a hard time finding it," the man said, standing near the open doorway now.

Then they came in.

"This is my wife, Angel." I felt stiff, like one of Vernon's statues.

"Pleased to meet you," and he shook my hand and smiled.

Then he saw the children, and he didn't say anthing, just kinda stared.

"This is our family," Vernon said so proudly, then introduced each child, telling the library man about their author godparents—and the library man thought it was the finest idea he had ever heard.

Vernon liked him. He knew so much about everything, especially art.

So, from that day on, every month, library man brought us our supply of books and stayed for supper.

Children loved him. They weren't frightened, not once they knew he knew their godparents.

Even I started talking to him. He was a kind man—like Vernon.

Somehow he knew we didn't have much money, with Vernon laid off. Tried to get Vernon to sell his work. No way.

I wouldn't sell my sewing either.

Then he suggested we sell our honey—

We'd never thought of that before.

There were so many flowers around our place—Vernon wanted to share with the bees. So we put in hives. And the bees had so much honey, they didn't mind sharing with us.

I'd make up special jellies, always using flowers—violets, nasturtiums—floating them in the clear jelly.

Vernon always praised me for my flower raising.

"Everyone has the ability within them to create something beautiful in this world—and if they can't do it alone, they can help God do it," he said. My planting flowers everywhere was only helping God.

So I started making extra batches of jellies and preserves. The library man, he drew labels. He was an artist with flowers, had a way of making the colors dance.

And he'd sell them for us. I didn't want to charge much—flowers and honey were gifts to us. But it did bring in some money.

We didn't need much to live on.

Eating—had given up eating meat long ago. Vernon didn't like killing anything.

"We're here to make things grow," he'd say. "Nature takes care of the dying—" He always believed in the cycles of life—time to live—time to die—

We grew our own vegetables. Oh and about once or twice a year, we'd lay in a supply of ground wheat—for bread, cereals.

Made our own wine too—from dandelions, chokecherries, and honey.

Library man wanted to sell our wine too—"Nectar of the gods," he'd say as he drank a toast with us.

Vernon didn't want to sell it, afraid people might drink too much.

"A man is always responsible for what he creates," he'd say, "be it children, problems, or his pieces of work—"

Then—that one winter—snowed so hard—bitter cold. Library man got penumonia.

In spring, he sent somebody else up with the books. Vernon, he didn't like this other person. Didn't even invite him in. The man kept asking about the children. Vernon just talked to him outside.

He could tell what people were like, just by being in their presence. Had that ability, look right through someone, see everything about them—good and bad.

Next month Vernon went down to see the library man. Took him a little scene he had carved. A man sitting under a tree, reading a book.

Oh, and the library man cried so, because he had never received such a beautiful gift.

Library man died that year.

That seemed the year everything started changing.

Vernon's arthritis got worse. His beautiful hands—gnarled— knots in them. Hurt me to look, like I could feel his pain. We were that close, we could feel one another's feelings.

Factory retired him early too—on a small pension.

His eyesight was starting to dim.

Even so, he could still turn out beauty. Crippled hands, dim eyes—some inner instinct seemed to guide him in his carving. At the end—that's what he did mostly, carving. Sitting at this window—so often looking into the distance—as if he were seeing and hearing things out there somewhere.

Me—I never seemed to change. Never sick, not since that one time. I still sewed. Gardened. Oh, I stopped making all those jellies—once the library man left. We let the bees go too.

"They served us long enough," Vernon said. And we made no more wine. There were no more toasts—

One night, we were in bed together, talking late like we always did, only Vernon seemed different. I could feel an innner trembling in him.

"Angel," he said, "I must tell you something—something I feel, so deep within, I can't contain it any longer."

Somehow I didn't want to hear.

"I always thought I'd be around, to protect you, take care of you," he started again. "You are the only woman I have ever loved—I always thought—you and I and the children, we'd grow old together—and we have . . . "

"But," he paused for such a long time, "I don't think I'm going to make it much longer . . . I think I'll be leaving before you do . . . "

"Don't talk like that," I cried out. Then the tears just flowed and flowed—the thought of being without Vernon.

But it happened anyway.

The Lord didn't make our lives come out even.

One night, it was the spring of the year, everything was budding, beginning new life again—

We went to bed early. Vernon kissed me, said, "I love you, Angel." Then he held my hand, like he did every night, only this night he held it so hard, like he didn't ever want to let go.

In the morning—his hand was cold . . .

His face looked so peaceful, like he was still sleeping. But he wasn't. The life force from inside him was gone.

It was raining outside. As if the whole world was crying.

I didn't know what to do . . .

I stayed at his bedside all day long. The tears wouldn't stop. The rain didn't stop. Terrible storm—lightning—thunder— the trees swaying, bending to the ground—everything crying out against the death of this very special man . . .

The children—they knew too. I could see each one of them crying . . .

I sat there, just thinking about our life together.

The beautiful things he had made . . .

How he said the good we did lived after us—

It didn't. It wouldn't! Not without him . . .

The moon came up, falling across our bed—where we lay together so many years. I couldn't watch there anymore.

I went outside. Dug a hole in the middle of the Magic Circle.

Then I took the quilt I was still making, from the embroidered pieces of his shirts, and I wrapped his lifeless body in it.

Somehow, I carried him to that hole.

One last look—

He—he—looked so quiet—stiff—still. Like one of his statues.

Only, his eyes were closed. His soul was gone . . .

I—I lay the earth over him.

With each shovelful I screamed out to God—to the whole universe.

"Why! Why!! Did you take him from me!"

But there was no one there to hear me.

For the first time, since Vernon and I met—I was alone . . . Truly alone.

I lay on his grave all night. Whispers of spring ghosts mocking all around me.

Sunrise, I dug a small pine tree, planted it atop. Something living had to grow from his death.

After—days and nights were the same. One long continuous pain . . .

Then one day, the mailman came up. Pounding on the door.

I talked to him outside. Mail had piled up, he said, so he was checking.

I tried telling him what happened—and that now I was left alone—with 27 children.

I don't remember all that happened after . . .

All I remember is that it was hot—so terribly hot. Everything dried up. Nothing grew in the garden.

His statues stood there. Circling his grave. Markers. Reminders.

One of those days . . . The sheriff and his men came up . . .

"Where is he?" they asked.

"Who?"— "Your husband?"

All I could do was point.

They dug him up. Shovels slapping in the dust.

I looked— I had to—

It was horrible. The quilt, that beautiful rainbow quilt—torn—shredded—and the smell—

Vernon lied, he said the good we did lived after us . . . There was nothing good in that grave . . . Nothing living anymore.

They took him away.

I screamed out—"No! No!! He has to stay here! Heavenly Hill is his home—he belongs with his family! . . . We still need him . . . "

Sheriff said he couldn't stay buried there. Was against the law.

Kept asking me all kinds of questions. My head was going dizzy.

They thought—he thought—maybe I killed Vernon—

"No! I loved him—I loved him," I kept screaming, long after they took him away.

The pine tree died.

Statues hovered like sceptres. Children didn't smile anymore.

Everything was mixed up— Couldn't get back to the patterns of daily life anymore—not without Vernon. Our lives had been so intertwined.

Then one day, some different men came up, because I didn't answer their letters. Said they had a will, signed by Vernon, given to the library man, to give to the museum people.

They read it aloud to me, outside, in the Magic Circle.

"Upon my death, all my pieces of work are to be given to the Mountain Valley Museum . . . "

I didn't hear all the rest. Vernon had told me about a will— once—I had forgotten . . .

They started walking around outside. Poking at his statues. Talking among themselves.

I wouldn't let them in the house, but they saw the children anyway, through the window.

"Look at those unusual pieces," one man said, pointing at the children.

"Keep away," I screamed. "Those aren't for you—those are *my* children . . .

"Will says all his art pieces go to the museum—"

"They're not going anywhere! They're mine! Everything in this house he made for me—No one else!"

They talked quiet among themselves.

"All right," they said. "Everything in the house will be considered personal gifts."

"We're going to have a hard time finding room for all this junk out here anyway . . . " one of them said.

"These pieces aren't junk," another said. "They were created by a very fine artist . . . "

Few days later, they came and hauled Vernon's statues away, one by one. Tore them right off the land. It was as if they had grown roots into the ground, standing there for such a long time.

I thought I heard them scream out—or was it me—or was it Vernon—

All I had left was the children now.

I double locked the whole house.

And I wouldn't go outside, unless I was sure nobody was coming up that pathway. My statues weren't there to guard me anymore.

The children were frightened too. So I hid you, in the basement, way back in the fruit cellar. I only let you out one at a time. There were too many to hide every time I thought someone might be coming.

It wasn't healthy for you down there—Cold—Damp. You began to get sick—smell funny.

But I didn't know what else to do. With Vernon gone. I just couldn't seem to do things right. He wasn't there to guide me anymore.

People kept coming.

I never opened the door.

Some shouted through the window.

"We want to talk to you—about your husband . . . He's a famous artist now."

"We want to interview you—for an art magazine."

"Is any more of his work for sale?"

"Go away!" I screamed, day after day. "Leave me alone—I don't want to talk to anyone . . . "

I put KEEP OUT signs all over.

One day, I was sitting alone in the Magic Circle—this lady—somehow, she sneaked up, stood in front of me.

I cried out.

"Don't be frightened," she said, so gently—and I wasn't.

"My name is Anne Lindsay. Can I talk to you for a minute?"

I felt frozen.

Talk? I missed talking—Vernon, and I, we talked every evening.

"Yes, I'll talk," I said.

She inquired about the children. How they were doing. She seemed really interested. Didn't call them pieces of art.

"Can I see them?" she asked.

How she said it—I wasn't afraid of her. So, I let her into the house. Two of the children were up from the basement.

"What lovely children," she exclaimed over them.

"How well dressed—what nice manners . . . "

Something wasn't right. I said they had to rest. I liked her there, yet, I didn't.

She asked if she might come again.

I hesitated—the old fright returning.

"I want to help you," she said, and her eyes looked sincere.

Help? I needed help—from somebody.

A week later, she came again . . . We talked.

"Can I see all the children now?" she asked.

I didn't want to bring them up. So, I took her down in the basement. They didn't look their best down there—

"That's a lot of children to care for," she said.

"Yes, yes it is. Especially without a husband."

"I want to help you," she said.

I needed help, but—

"I'm from the Welfare Department—"

Welfare Department! They were the people who had put me in the orphanage. Something fearful was rising in me again.

"I want to make sure you are taken care of—have enough funds to live on."

Funds? Money was almost gone. Vernon's pension checks stopped coming after he died. Canister money was near bottom . . .

"If you'd just fill out some of these reports—"

"What reports?" It started getting confusing again.

"Stating you are without funds—we can give you emergency assistance. But for any general assistance—well, you couldn't retain anything of great value."

"I have nothing of great value—"

"Your children—they're priceless—great art treasures."

"My children?"

"Yes, if you ever really need money, you can always sell them—" She was pointing at Evangeline.

"Sell my children! Never! Never!!"

"Well, maybe someday you'll change your mind."

"I won't! You can leave now!" I yelled at her, "And don't ever come back!"

After that, I never left the place—not even to go to the store. I couldn't leave you alone. Now that she knew your hiding place.

I put barbed wire across the path. More big signs.

I'd hear noises at ngiht. See faces/eyes, peering from the trees. Wait—

Goes to window.

Somebody's out there now!

What if they came for you? What if today is the day?

No, it's only a bush . . .

I'm afraid—so afraid . . .

Sits ands rocks, arms hugging her stomach. Singing in broken rhythms.

"Hush little baby, don't you cry—
Papa's gonna be here bye and bye . . . "

Looks up, different mood prevailing.

You're my comfort, you know—my last child—for my old age.
I didn't know you'd be the last—Did he know—

Oh, you remind me so much of Vernon. You have Vernon's
eyes—Vernon's smile—

And when you sit in Vernon's chair like that, wearing Vernon's
clothes—it's—just as if Vernon was sitting there . . .

Sits.

And I can sit and talk to you, like Vernon and I used to.

I would read to him . . . Stories . . . Poems . . .

Back in recollection. Slowly as if remembering.

"There was a time when meadow, grove and stream,
The earth and every common sight,
   To me did seem
Apparelled in celestial light—
The glory and the freshness of a dream.
It is not now as it hath been of yore;
   Turn wheresoe'r I may,
   By night or day
The things which I have seen I can see no more . . . "

Turns to figure. Change of mood. Addressing him as Vernon.

That's all I remember, Vernon—

It's so hard to remember things lately.

I get the children mixed too . . .

It's getting dark out there, Vernon.

Owls are calling, "Whooo Whooo."

I don't know who . . .

Pause. More urgent.

Vernon, I've got to talk to you.

You've got to tell me what to do.

All right—I'll be calm—Just listen—I didn't want to tell you, but I have to tell somebody.

A bit slower.

The garden's gone, Vernon. Weeds. Only weeds. I can't—I can't work out there anymore. Your statues—they went—somewhere . . .

I can't get to the store anymore—I forgot the way . . .

Food—I don't know what happened to it—where I hid it—we always had so much.

Children are hungry. Crying all the time.

—And the mail. I didn't tell you about the mail, did I? I don't go down to get it every day. When I do, it's stacked up—

I open things, but I'm not sure what they're for.

Vernon, please, you have to start doing the mail again. I—I—don't want to anymore . . .

Those people—you want to know about those people—I don't like to worry you—so I didn't tell you—they were sheriff people—came again—the other day—I don't remember which day . . .

They said I didn't answer their tax leter.

I didn't know there was a tax letter.

You didn't tell me . . .

Taxes on this house, this land—they must be paid, in one month, that's what they said—or I couldn't live here anymore.

Where would we live then, Vernon? Where??

Welfare lady came again too.

Kept asking if we had enough food. I wouldn't speak to her . . .

She said she talked to the museum—they were willing to take the children—give them a good home. Pay me—

"I can't sell my children!" I screamed at her.

"They need food," she said.

"I need food too—" and I began to cry. Tears wouldn't stop.

"The museum will take good care of them—"

"No!"

"You could visit them anytime you wanted–"

"No! Nooo . . . "

"Twenty seven children are too many for any mother."

"Noooo . . . "

"What will happen when your house is taken? Where will your children go then?"

Breaks down.

"Go away! Go away and leave me alone . . . "

Gets up. Walks to window. Sits down.

What are we going to do, Vernon? Tell me—

What? You *want* me to sell the children—

No! No!!

Whispers.

Yes—, yes, I'll calm down and listen.

What? I can't hear you so well anymore . . .

As if listening. Pause.

I—I must take one child—only one—and give it to the musuem. Then they will pay my taxes—give me money for food—

Which one Vernon? Which one must I part with!!

The baby? Our first?

No—

Each year, give one child only. Then I wouldn't miss them as much.

One each year—for twenty seven years—

Crying.

I can't do it, Vernon—I can't.

I know—I know other children grow up—leave home. But these are special children. Afraid of strangers. At the museum—those people would be staring at them, poking at them.

And they'd be so lonely, without us. Lonely for each other . . . As lonely as I would be if I were ever without you . . .

What?

They should all go together then? So they won't be separated, can care for one another.

I don't know—I don't know what to do . . . Children—they don't like it in the basement . . .

One? Couldn't I keep just one?

The last one, Vernon. The one you never finished. I can keep that one, can't I—to talk to, read to—

They wouldn't want an unfinished child anyway— Then we can stay on Heavenly Hill—together.

Looking into distance. More vague.

The museum people are coming tomorrow—or was it yesterday—I don't know, things have become confused lately . . .

You—you tell them, the children, Vernon. I don't want to be the one.

We'll go to bed early tonight. Get them up before sunrise. Dress them. Feed them. Pack their clothes . . .

They'll cry— I know they'll cry . . .

"Everybody has to leave—sometime. It's a pattern of life."

But not you—don't you ever leave . . .

I—I guess I could stand them being gone— Promise—promise you'll stay with me—always!

Reaches out, takes hand of figure.

I—I don't know what I'd do without you, Vernon. I just don't know . . .

Or this house. And all the lovely things you made me.

Gets up. Walks around.

That table. Roses twining around the legs . . .

This chair, polished like silk—always feels like arms holding me.

And that chest, cedar smell stays with it—always—and the scent of your body, when you made it—that's always there too.

Things can be gone—and still be here, can't they . . .

You're always here—through your work—your love . . . It's as if the whole house were always lit by your presence . . .

I'm glad you didn't pass on before me . . .

One time you said you would. But I didn't want you to—my wishing was so strong—it kept you here.

Sits. Conversational.

It's getting dark outside now, Vernon. So very dark.

Moon will be hitting these windows soon.

It's time we were getting to bed, don't you think . . .

Goes to pick up figure

Come, I'll rub your legs for you again tonight. So the arthritis doesn't hurt so bad.

And tomorrow—we can go visit the children. And the library man too. We haven't seen him for such a long time . . .

Picks up figure. Stands. Looks out the window.

Such a beautiful sight.

All your statues. Standing in rows like that. Works of eternity. That's what you call them, don't you—

Works of eternal love . . .

LIGHTS DIM—CURTAIN

PRODUCTION NOTES

Lifesize doll is important to production, but need not be a hindrance.

Body of doll can be made from an old night gown, stuffed with a huge pillow, tied at waist (for bendability). Rolled towels can fill out the arms and stuffed gloves for hands.

Head can be an inexpensive styrofoam head used to hold wigs. It can be sculpted, painted to resemble wood.

Doll is seated or held, so legs need not be apparent.

Experimentation can bring interesting results, since this is a "carved" doll—but the intent to make it "alive" should also be apparent.

Late/Late . . . Computer Date

CHARACTERS:

ISOBEL *(Late 60's)*
VERONICA *(Early 60's)*

TIME: *The Present*

PLACE: *The sitting room of the Paisley Sisters*

SETTING: *A roomful of clutter and memorabilia. Small table center with lace cloth, framed photos, tarnished gold music box, and half empty tea cups. Chairs on either side.*

Stage right is a folding screen crowded with photos, picture postcards, programs and other souvenirs. Stage left is a parrot on a stand. He's real looking, but we're never sure whether he's alive, atrophied, or stuffed. An apron covers him.

Scene opens:

ISOBEL *enters in a frenzy, carrying a boxful of items and a sewing basket. She is wearing an old faded dressing gown from another era, over it a white smock with "MISS LILLY'S PURE CANDIES" embroidered across the back.*

She sets down her paraphenalia and begins arranging items about. Notices parrot.

ISOBEL: My, my—did we forget to uncover Admiral Bird today too. *(Removes apron)* Forgive us Admiral, we've just been so busy—A regular circus it's been around here . . .

There, now you can watch what's going on too. See how pretty Veronica looks this evening. None of your wisecracks though. She's upset enough. Takes so little to upset her lately.

Oh dear, no one's pulled the shades up either. And already it's time to pull them down . . .

Veronica? Are you coming along in here? There isn't that much time, and there's lots more we have to do with you.

VERONICA: *(Offstage)* I'm coming.

ISOBEL: You're going to be late as usual.

VERONICA *enters, carrying one shoe. She's wearing a full length pale peach lace formal. A large sash is tied in a bow at the side. Her curly blond hair, which looks obviously wiglike, has a peach ribbon in it. Spots of rouge and bowlike mouth are part of her strange makeup.*

VERONICA: I can't move any faster in this long dress— skyscraper shoes—

ISOBEL: *(Still arranging things. Trying to maintain partylike atmosphere)* Your own fault. I told you all week long to practice. "Practice," I said, "Practice walking in those new shoes, because Saturday night, that big, big night is coming up awfully soon!" *(Begins puttering in wicker sewing basket)*

VERONICA: I wish it had never come. *(Plops into chair right, "her" chair)* My feet hurt. My head itches. I don't know why you made me wear this wig.

ISOBEL: Because you're getting gray . . . And growing bald too.

VERONICA: I am not.

ISOBEL: Well, you don't see the top of your head like I do. Stand up now, so I can sew some flowers over those worn spots. *(Begins sewing small cloth flowers at random on the dress)*

VERONICA: A computer dance doesn't seem a very suitable place to be wearing mama's wedding gown.

Not since we took off all the ruffles. Dyed it a nice apricot.

VERONICA: Apricot? Looks more like dead pumpkin to me—or rotten squash!

ISOBEL: We're going to be pleasant tonight, aren't we.

VERONICA: Nobody'll be wearing long dresses.

ISOBEL: You should be proud to be wearing mama's wedding gown. All these years it's been saved—for you—for that special someday . . . And well, since it didn't look like that someday was on the horizon—tonight seemed the perfect occasion.

VERONICA: Wig'll probably fall off while I'm dancing—then what'll I do?

ISOBEL: Can't possibly. We sewed it to your own hair even.

VERONICA: —And I'll probably fall too. In these tipsy shoes. Why didn't you let me wear my Sunday oxfords?—Or old tennies?

ISOBEL: Because, he's a foot taller than you. That's why. We want you matching him as closely as possible.

VERONICA: Computer Suitor was supposed to do that. That wonderful monster matching machine.

ISOBEL: Well, it's not that easy—finding you a date. Not in your age bracket. Took them two whole years to even find you this one.

VERONICA: I wish they hadn't.

ISOBEL: Well, they did. And you're going through with it!

VERONICA: I wish the machine had broken down—Or given up—Or blown a fuse!

ISOBEL: Once you get there, you'll enjoy it, I'm sure.

VERONICA: If you're so sure, why don't you go in my place.

ISOBEL: —Just like all those other things you never wanted to attend. Plays. Concerts. And once you got there, why you enjoyed them even more than anybody. *(Finishes sewing)*

VERONICA: Those were different, Isobel. I could just sit there. I didn't have to do anything.

ISOBEL: *(Stands back to survey dress)* And the trips . . . Why I remember that first one, couldn't even get your near the train, kicking and screaming. Then, after, why you enjoyed those yearly trips even more than I did.

VERONICA: *(Walking away)* Because nobody knew us. And I could pretend to be somebody else.

But tonight, my computer date, he knows everything about me. And I won't be able to pretend anything. I'll have to be just me.

ISOBEL: *(Scanning items on memory screen)* Think what you would have missed if I hadn't made you go that first time.

Yellowstone National Park . . . Cypress Gardens . . . Painted Desert . . . Redwood Forest . . . Disneyland . . .

VERONICA: *(Out of her reverie)* Disneyland! Oh, that's one place I'd really like to go back to—Fairytale Land—Fantasy Land . . .

ISOBEL: Tonight, the dance, it'll be just like Fantasy Land.

VERONICA: You're just saying that.

ISOBEL: No. For my prom they had the whole gym decorated like an underwater garden . . . "King Neptune's Fantasy Land" they called it . . . Seas of green crepe paper. Silver mermaids . . .

But, there's no time for memories now, not with all that still has to be done.

(Digs out old furpiece from box, shakes it, dust flies) Mama's fur hasn't been worn for such a long time. Still smells of moth balls too. *(Begins brushing it)*

VERONICA: You've been on a date before—your senior prom. You'd know much better what to do.

ISOBEL: Yes, I've had my date. And now it's your turn, Veronica.

VERONICA: But, I never wanted a date. Honest. I've always been frightened around men.

ISOBEL: Nonsense. Everyone should have a date. At least once before they die. And I've promised you one for such a long time. *(Up)* That sash still hangs crooked. *(Straightens it)*

VERONICA: It still feels tight.

ISOBEL: Course it feels tight. Stuffing yourself all week on Miss Lilly's Candies.

VERONICA: Don't even mention candy—

ISOBEL: Poor garbagemen. What are they going to think when they come looking for their boxes of candy?
Every week for the past three years, ever since we retired from the candy factory, those two pension boxes of Miss Lilly's Chocolates have been sitting there, right on top of the garbage cans—
Because, you didn't want them in the house. Didn't want to be reminded of the candy factory. You had given up eating candy. Forever!

VERONICA: I was so nervous—all week.

ISOBEL: Poor garbagemen—they'll wonder what happened.

VERONICA: We were never sure if they ate the candy or not.

ISOBEL: Boxes were gone every week.

VERONICA: So was the garbage.

ISOBEL: Little enough reward for them, coming down this long empty road. Ours the only house on it.

VERONICA: They wouldn't have to come at all anymore.

ISOBEL: You don't want anyone here anymore—

VERONICA: That's not the reason—

ISOBEL: Running and hiding everytime you hear a car motoring down that loose gravel.

VERONICA: I'm not afraid of the garbagemen. I'm never afraid of people in uniform. Because I know who they are.

ISOBEL: Then, why did you say they didn't have to come anymore. I can't make sense out of anything you say lately—
(Picks up fur piece again.)

VERONICA: If you wouldn't interrupt all the time—

ISOBEL: Wouldn't you know, moth holes in it too. Well, maybe I can quick sew them together.

VERONICA: —They don't have to come here, because there's hardly any garbage anymore. All that's in the can lately is empty newspapers from underneath Admiral Bird.
And pretty soon you'll be adding those to your mulch pile too.

ISOBEL: Nothing wrong in being thrifty.

VERONICA: You save everything. Way past its time. Even Admiral Bird—he's been silent for years.

ISOBEL: Only when you're around. He speaks to me on many occasions.

VERONICA: Basement floor's filled with empty glass jars and bottles. We'll never use them up even if we make dandelion wine and apple butter the rest of our lives.
And every year we make less and less, because the apples are getting wormier and wormier.

ISOBEL: What are you ranting on about now, when I'm trying to thread this needle.

VERONICA: —And the tin cans. Thousands of washed empty tin cans. Half of them rusting away, because you're saving them for planting tomatoes—or mixing paint, or whatever.

ISOBEL: I'm sorry. I'm the one who has to watch the pennies around here. See that our pension money lasts the rest of our

lives . . . And, since we don't know how long that's going to
be—

VERONICA: If you're so worried about money, you didn't have
to waste two hundred dollars on this computer date!

ISOBEL: Enough! *(Bang is heard. Both jump)*
(Trills) Paper boy! Stay still, it's *my* turn to get it tonight.

VERONICA: Why does he always bang it against the screen
door. I keep thinking someone's trying to get in—

ISOBEL: *(Leaving)* I've told him time and again, but—

VERONICA: I think he resents having to come down our long
empty road too. The only customer on it.
(To herself) Maybe we should leave him a box of chocolates
too. And the mailman. He hardly leaves any mail anymore.
Only our pension check. Once a month. .
Paper. Pension. And two boxes of chocolates. That's all that
comes here anymore.

ISOBEL: *(Bringing in paper. Scanning)* Obituaries—page three.
No, no one we know died. That's always a relief.

VERONICA: Because everyone we know's dead already.

ISOBEL: You always say that, and then somebody we forgot
about up and dies.

VERONICA: The weather? Maybe there's severe weather warn-
ings, telling people to stay home tonight.

ISOBEL: No. It's going to be a lovely warm evening. And,
there's even going to be a full moon. What do you think of that!

VERONICA: Won't matter. We'll be inside anyway.

ISOBEL: *(Teasing)* What about when he takes you home?

VERONICA: Takes me home? I thought the dance was the only
part.

ISOBEL: If he's your date—he takes you home.

VERONICA: *(Panicky)* But, I planned on taking a taxi—

ISOBEL: His Match-A-Chart even said he had a Chrysler coupe!

VERONICA: Read me again, what his Match-A-Chart says—

ISOBEL: Good Lord, Veronica, we've gone over that Match-A-Chart must be a hundred times.

VERONICA: But I can't remember a thing right now.

ISOBEL: All right. Very quickly then. There's still things we have to do. Time's racing by. *(Gets chart from pile by table)*

VERONICA: *(Panicky)* His name—What's his name again?

ISOBEL: Arthur McIntosh. Just remember, like the apple.

VERONICA: That's no good. There's Jonathan apples too.

ISOBEL: Arthur! For apple!

VERONICA: His age? What's his age again?

ISOBEL: Let's see—He has down—"over seventy".

VERONICA: That means he could be eighty, or even ninety.

ISOBEL: Well, you put down "over fifty", didn't you?

VERONICA: You did, you mean. You filled out my Match-A-Chart.

ISOBEL: Only because you refused to.

VERONICA: I've never told my age to anyone— *(Begins scratching arms)*

ISOBEL: You're getting nervous again. And perspiring. Will you sit still, and stop perspiring.

VERONICA: I can't help it.

ISOBEL: You're going to get that gown all sweaty.
And, remember to spray on deoderant again, just before you leave.

VERONICA: I've put on five different brands already.

ISOBEL: So, one of them should work.

VERONICA: What else? About— *(Remembers)* Arthur?

ISOBEL: —"Occupation: Former Baker."

VERONICA: I won't know what to say to a baker.

ISOBEL: You can—talk about your work at the candy factory.

VERONICA: I haven't worked there for over three years.

ISOBEL: Good Lord, Veronica, after forty years, you should have something to say about the place.

VERONICA: But not to anyone else. I never spoke to anyone else about the candy factory. That was our world. Yours and mine.

ISOBEL: Well, it's gone now. Everything . . .
"Hobbies: Collects paperweights."

VERONICA: What if he talks about paperweights?

ISOBEL: Talk with him.

VERONICA: But, you put down I collected paperweights too.

ISOBEL: Yes. And I'm sure that's why they matched you two. Seems the only thing you both had in common.

VERONICA: But, I don't collect paperweights.

ISOBEL: We had to give you some hobby.

VERONICA: I collect candy boxes.

ISOBEL: That's not a "regular" hobby.

VERONICA: You shouldn't have lied, Isobel. You told so many lies on my sheet.

ISOBEL: They were not lies, Veronica. Only stretches of the truth a bit. You do have two paperweights.

VERONICA: But, I don't collect them.

ISOBEL: Where did you get them from, if you didn't collect them?

VERONICA: Enough from the chart. It only seems to upset me more.

ISOBEL: Every little thing seems to upset you lately. *(Puts chart back on table. Begins rummaging through box)*
Well, after tonight, when things get back to normal around here—

VERONICA: Isobel—I don't feel well. And I'm not faking this time. My stomach—

ISOBEL: I told you they don't refund the money. You have to go! Or we lose everything!

VERONICA: My insides are churning—

ISOBEL: *(More concerned)* Would you like some more sassafras tea?

VERONICA: No! There's a tidal wave of tea rolling round inside me right now.

ISOBEL: *(Searching frantically through the box)* Smelling salts? We'll give you some smelling salts.

VERONICA: No! Nothing to eat or smell. Not right now!

ISOBEL: *(Flustered)* Relax—Just try to relax then.

VERONICA: I keep thinking about tonight.

ISOBEL: Well, don't—

VERONICA: All these months. All these preparations. And, now, it's finally here . . .

ISOBEL: *(Claps hands)* I know! Let's play "Happy Memory Time"!

VERONICA: Not right now.

ISOBEL: We have to do something to keep you from thinking about the dance.

VERONICA: All right. Anything to calm my stomach.

Isobel: I'll be the leader this time. *(Sits)*
Close your eyes. Let your head float . . . float . . . Up into the sky . . . And think back . . . think back to happy times . . .

Veronica: *(Presses fingertips against her temples and begins rocking motion)* I'm thinking. Very hard.

Isobel: Think back to mama. When mama was still living . . .

Veronica: It gets harder and harder to remember mama.

Isobel: You're a tiny baby now . . . Mama's putting you in your little bed. A tiny pink bed with rosebuds and teensy elves all over it . . .
Now mamma's putting on her long silky robe, the one with huge orange poppies . . . She sits at her harpsichord, and begins plucking the strings. The whole house fills with harpsichord music . . .

Veronica: *(Suddenly frightened)* I don't want to remember mama . . . Not now . . .

Isobel: You agreed—

Veronica: *(Out of her memory position)* The candy factory. Talk about the candy factory.

Isobel: You always ask for the candy factory.

Veronica: Because it had so many pleasant memories . . . And I don't know why we had to leave there.

Isobel: Because I had to retire when I was 65. That's why!

Veronica: But, I wasn't 65—

Isobel: Are we going to play the memory game or not?

Veronica: It works better when I do the leading.

Isobel: All right. But then, next time, it's my turn.

Veronica: *(Back in position)* I'm a little girl now . . . My hair is swinging in long golden curls, and I'm wearing a huge pink bow . . . It matches my pink dress, with rows and rows of gathered ruffles around the skirt . . .

And I'm going to the library. I go to the library every Monday, and pick out fairytale books . . .

I'm inside now. Looking through the shelves . . . I see one with a bright pink cover. It matches my dress. I pull it from the shelf. "MARY LOU IN CANDYLAND". Inside are colored pictures of Candyland. Everything is made of candy . . . Peppermint canes . . . Lollipops . . . Chocolate Creams . . . And, I want to go there. I want to run off with Mary Lou . . . *(Pause)*

ISOBEL: Go on, please. Or are you through?

VERONICA: No . . .

It's my first day at the candy factory . . . I have on my white smock with "Miss Lilly's Pure Candies" embroidered across the back . . . I hold your hand, we walk through the door, into the factory. And there's candy everywhere . . . Tables and tables . . . And, it's just like being in the storybook Candyland . . .

And, then Miss Lilly enters—

ISOBEL: *(Interrupts)* That's enough! Enough memories right now.

We really don't have the time. We just wanted to calm you down some. That's all. *(Sips her tea)*

VERONICA: *(Rubbing her eyes)* I should have stayed at the candy factory.

ISOBEL: They were just keeping us on as a favor anyway. Why, we were the only two hand chocolate dippers left. Once we retired, our job was automated. Like everything else.

VERONICA: I miss it, Isobel.

ISOBEL: So do I. So do I . . .

VERONICA: That was our place in life, wasn't it. Everyone has a place in life, and that was ours. And they made us leave it. Like being banished from Paradise.

ISOBEL: Well, once Miss Lilly left, things were never quite the same.

VERONICA: Sold out, you mean. Sold out her precious candy company to that big, big concern.

ISOBEL: *(Sets down cup)* Enough reminiscing.
(Up) Time's wasting. Let's see—Oh Lord, we still have to put on your nail polish. *(Rummages through box)*

VERONICA: I hate nail polish.

ISOBEL: You need something to cover those ugly bitten nails. Even worse this week. Just look at them. *(Shakes hand in her face)*

VERONICA: I can't see. Because you won't let me wear my glasses.

ISOBEL: One night without them won't hurt. You look younger and better without them. *(Begins putting on polish)*

VERONICA: Look better, but not see better. I won't even be able to tell what this Arthur really looks like.

ISOBEL: You've seen his photo.

VERONICA: Years old probably. Like my picture you sent him.

ISOBEL: It was all we had—

VERONICA: Me, waving from Pike's Peak.

ISOBEL: I thought it showed an adventurous spirit.

VERONICA: Adventurous! I was waving for help.

ISOBEL: Well, you won't let your photo be taken, unless it's at some scenic spot.

VERONICA: You'll be asking me how he looks, and I won't be able to tell you. Because I won't be able to see.

ISOBEL: Look here, Veronica, we went through all this two years ago, when I first answered that Computer Suitor ad on TV—We discussed then whether to get you contact lenses or false teeth for this date, with the rest of your insurance settlement from mama and daddy's accident. And, we decided false teeth was more important.

VERONICA: You decided. I didn't want either.

ISOBEL: You couldn't go on a date with such rotten teeth. All those years of eating candy. Always a sucker in your mouth. Wore a hole in that spot even.

VERONICA: I liked my old teeth—

ISOBEL: You look much better now, with a full mouthful of nice white teeth.

VERONICA: *(Pushing at teeth)* They still don't fit right.

ISOBEL: Why didn't you mention it to Dr. Shishedo last visit?

VERONICA: It's difficult enough for me to talk to men. But sitting in a dentist's chair is even worse. Especially when he speaks mostly in Japanese.

ISOBEL: He charges less.

VERONICA: Only time I'm really comfortable, is at night. While those teeth are sitting in their glass of water on the dresser, I smile all the time.
And, all night long, I'm somebody else. Not the same person as in the daytime.

ISOBEL: Oh, you've always been that way. Two different types of people.

VERONICA: Well, I never looked two different ways. And now with my teeth I can.

ISOBEL: Those were expensive teeth. Imported—from Japan.
(Up) Sit still now till those nails dry.

VERONICA: We should have spent that money on one great grand glorious trip!

ISOBEL: Oh no. Every penny from that terrible automobile accident—all those years of your wearing a neck brace—every penny was spent for your personal improvement. Things mama would have wanted for you. Had she lived. Ballet lessons. Singing lessons—

VERONICA: But, I never wanted any of them.

ISOBEL: I promised mama, at the hospital—she could barely talk—that I would take care of you.

And I promised myself, the insurance settlement, all ten thousand dollars, would be spent only for your benefit.

All those years of lessons, concerts, plays—till there was only four hundred left.

So, two hundred was set aside for this computer date. And two hundred for new teeth.

Now the money's gone. My job is finished. My conscience is clear. *(Sits)*

VERONICA: I still would rather have gone on a trip.

ISOBEL: There are no more trips! Because there is no more Christmas bonus for trips! No more money at all, except our pension checks, which barely covers living expenses.

VERONICA: Couldn't we sell mama and daddy's house—we only use part anyway, buy a trailer, and just travel all over.

ISOBEL: More impractical dreams. Besides, we've seen just about every place in this country worth seeing.

VERONICA: Not the new Disneyland. The one in Florida.

ISOBEL: Same as the other.

VERONICA: No, this one's supposed to be lots better.

ISOBEL: *(Dismissing)* I almost forgot. Foot powder. *(Gets shaker jar of powder from box and sprinkles on VERONICA's feet)* So your feet won't perspire while you're dancing.

VERONICA: *(Plaintively)* Isobel—could we, could we practice dancing? Just one more time?

ISOBEL: Not now.

VERONICA: You promised—

ISOBEL: We've been dancing around here all week.

VERONICA: Not in this long dress.

ISOBEL: All right. If it'll make you feel any better.
(Winds up music box. "Happy Birthday" plays)

VERONICA: Happy Birthday? But, that's not a waltz.

ISOBEL: *(Takes off her smock)* It'll have to do. I'm not wheeling out the victrola right now. Just do it waltz tempo, like we practiced. *(Bows and says in deep man's voice)* "May I have this dance, Miss Veronica?"

VERONICA: *(Curtsies. Stiff and nervous)* Yes. Yes—Arthur—

They dance awkwardly. ISOBEL counting, "One two, three." VERONICA nervously tries to follow. She stumbles

VERONICA: I can't do it! I just can't do it!

ISOBEL: You did it the other day.

VERONICA: I don't know why you're making me do this! Making me go places I don't want to. Do things I don't want to do. Always pushing me!

ISOBEL: *(Accusingly)* You've never appreciated anything I've done for you—

VERONICA: Don't start—

ISOBEL: Always so worried about yourself. Think what I've given up!

VERONICA: *(Puts hands over ears)* I don't want to hear all that again.

ISOBEL: A trip to Europe. With Miss Lilly. But, no, I stayed home so I could care for my sister. Nurse you through that one whole year—

VERONICA: I don't want to play that memory game!

ISOBEL: —Miss Lilly's traveling assistant. I could have been her assistant! Traveled all through the wonders of Europe with her.

VERONICA: You could have gone—put me in hospital.

ISOBEL: *(To her)* Hospital? When you have tuberculosis, you don't go to a hospital. They put you in a sanatorium, and you never get out. And no one can even come to visit you.

VERONICA: I still don't believe I had tuberculosis. You never had any tests made.

ISOBEL: And you know very well why. If a doctor had even suspected, they would have taken you away. Immediately.

VERONICA: I'm still certain it was a nervous breakdown. Like the time before—

ISOBEL: You were so ill that year—you don't remember anything.

VERONICA: Enough to realize that I felt just like that time before—When mama was still living. And she took me away . . . to that big gray stone building . . . and I made all those baskets . . .

ISOBEL: It was not the same!

VERONICA: In my head it was. Everything in my head was all mixed up . . . I try real hard some days, but I can never remember what went on those times . . . Like I was away from the world for awhile. And then I came back . . .

ISOBEL: You're not supposed to remember—The doctor said to keep you from dwelling on it. That's why we play the "Happy Memory Game."—to remember only the happy times.

VERONICA: *(Going into her own world)* Both times—they keep coming back. Pushing into my head . . .

ISOBEL: Shut them out!

VERONICA: The first time . . . *(Up)*
(Like she's reliving the event) The night of my ballet recital . . . Miss Maryknoll's Dancing Class . . . And I was this butterfly . . . And I was twirling and twirling, faster and faster— then suddenly I felt like I was going to spin off the edge of

the earth—and I started screaming and screaming, tearing off those butterfly wings, and those yards and yards of gauze that were choking me . . .

ISOBEL: Enough!

VERONICA: *(The panic building. Sits)* Tonight, Isobel, I feel the same way. Like I'm being crushed. Can't breathe—

ISOBEL: That all happened a long time ago. You've been all right for years now. Mama told me what to watch for.

ISOBEL: I don't tell you. Not all the time. Because I know how it upsets you. So, I go to my room and shut the door, till I get over it.
(Hysteria building) But tonight, I can't go to my room. I have to go away. Alone. Without you. With all these people. And be with a perfect stranger! *(Breaks into hysterical sobs)*

ISOBEL: *(Nearing hysteria too)* It's going to be all right! Everything will be all right!

VERONICA: *(Rocking and sobbing)* I don't want to go . . . Don't make me go . . .

ISOBEL: Wait. Wait! *(A last resort)* We'll give you your dandelion wine!

VERONICA: Mama . . . I don't want to go—

ISOBEL: *(Takes fruit jar from under table. Pours jelly glass full of yellow wine)* Here, Veronica. Drink down your dandelion wine. A nice long drink. (VERONICA *gulps between quieting sobs)*
Feel better now?

VERONICA: A little.

ISOBEL: In a few minutes you'll be all better. A little more?

VERONICA: *(Another sip)* That's enough. I feel better. Much better.

ISOBEL: *(Pours remaining wine back into jar and puts back under table)* I didn't want to use the wine. Not tonight. I wanted this memory to be so special. Wine always clouds up everything for you.

VERONICA: I would have started screaming, Isobel. And I know I couldn't have stopped.

ISOBEL: Sit back and relax. And I'll rub in that bleach cream. Fade those age spots some more.

VERONICA: I wish it could make me fade—far, far away.

ISOBEL: There. Your hands are warming too. Icyness going away. Far away. And pretty soon, you'll be all right.

VERONICA: I wish I could go to bed. Let my dreams take over . . .
Remember at the candy factory, when I used to tell you my dreams?

ISOBEL: Like clockwork, those dreams poured out of you. Every morning.

VERONICA: While we dipped bon bons. Pink . . . Yellow . . . Green . . .

ISOBEL: And this one morning, you swore it wasn't a dream. That there really had been little men sitting on your bed the night before.

VERONICA: And, you didn't believe me—

ISOBEL: How could I.

VERONICA: I never told you any more dreams after that.
You never understood my reason for collecting candy boxes either.

ISOBEL: Collecting, maybe. But sitting and staring at them for hours on end. Putting empty boxes up to your ear.

VERONICA: I don't stare at them. I smell them. And if I close my eyes, I can pretend I'm back at the candy factory.
And when I put the boxes up to my ear, it's like with a seashell, I can hear all the sounds of wherever the box has been.

ISOBEL: *(Up)* Oh, I almost forgot. My little surprise for you.

VERONICA: What now?

ISOBEL: Something much better than the scent of empty candy boxes. One minute, I'll be right back. *(Leaves)*

VERONICA: *(Puts candy box up to ear)* Where have you been little box? What stories can you tell me today? . . . I smell chocolate cherries. *(Hears* ISOBEL, *quickly puts box away)*

ISOBEL: *(Returns with small silver box)* Here it is. My special surprise—"Paris Nights".

VERONICA: Paris Nights?

ISOBEL: Yes. The perfume Miss Lilly sent me, from Paris. The European trip. The one I didn't go on—

VERONICA: That was thirty five years ago.

ISOBEL: Yes, and I've saved it, using only drops at a time, for special occasions. And tonight, I'm sharing it with you.

VERONICA: I never wear perfume—

ISOBEL: But, for the dance—

VERONICA: At the candy factory—Miss Lilly never allowed it.

ISOBEL: *(Has bottle out of box. Holds up like a crystal ball)* Ummmmm. All the scents of Paris, captured in this tiny crystal bottle . . . *(Takes off stopper, puts it up to* VERONICA'S *face)* Here, smell the aroma—

VERONICA: I told you I don't want any! *(Push bottle sharply away. Perfume spills and bottle falls)* Keep it away from me!

ISOBEL: *(Screaming)* Look what you did!

VERONICA: It's all over me! *(Tries to fight it off)*

ISOBEL: *(Retrieving bottle)* Spilled! Every drop!

VERONICA: All over mama's wedding gown!

ISOBEL: *(Turning visciously on her)* What's wrong with you! Why can't you act like normal people. *(VERONICA begins untying sash)* What are you doing?

VERONICA: Taking this gown off.

ISOBEL: You leave that dress on!

VERONICA: I won't go smelling like a Paris whorehouse!

ISOBEL: *(Grabs her by shoulders. Shakes her)* What do you mean, whorehouse!

VERONICA: Yes! That's what Miss Lilly smelled like—

ISOBEL: *(Walks away in a frenzy)* You don't know what you're saying!

VERONICA: *(Shouting at her)* Miss Lilly's Pure Candies! Hah! There was nothing pure about her. And everybody at the candy factory knew! Everybody—except you!

ISOBEL: Your mind is wandering again!

VERONICA: With all her fancy satins, and jewels, and furs—she was still nothing but a common whore!

ISOBEL: You're crazy! You always have been!

VERONICA: A common whore!

ISOBEL: You should have been put away long ago!

VERONICA: —And I won't go smelling like her! *(Tears off sash and throws it to the floor. Begins on dress)*

ISOBEL: *(No longer under control)* Destroy the dress then! Destroy everything! Everything!
(Whirls around. Goes to screen) All our other memories too. Who needs anything to remember. Tear up everything! Everything!
(Begins tearing things off screen, ripping them in two in a wild frenzy)

VERONICA: *(Horrified scream)* No! Not our souvenirs! *(Stands petrified)*

ISOBEL: *(Viciously)* Chicago World's Fair—No need to remember that glorous trip! *(Rips)* Yellowstone . . . Old Faith

ful . . . Tear them up! Tear everything up! Painted Desert . . .
Cypress Gardens . . .

VERONICA: I'll wear the dress. *(Breaks into sobs)*

ISOBEL: *(Continuing)* Get rid of everything! Everything from
the past, so it's not around to haunt us anymore.

VERONICA: I'll wear the dress—

ISOBEL: *(Turns to table and throws down photo of mama in cardboard
frame)* Everything old and dead! Get rid of it!

VERONICA: *(Screams)* Mama!

ISOBEL: Everything! *(Goes to parrot, grabs him. As she's about to
throw him)*

VERONICA: *(Screams)* Admiral Bird! Mama's wedding present!

ISOBEL: *(Shocked into her senses, stops in mid-throw)*
Admiral Bird—I'm sorry—

VERONICA: *(Sinks to floor. Sobbing and rocking)* Mama . . .
Mama . . . Help me!

ISOBEL: *(Coming back into focus)* I'm sorry Admiral Bird. I lost
control. I don't know what happened to me.

VERONICA: Mama . . . Take me away from here.

ISOBEL: *(Commanding voice again)* Stop crying, Veronica! You
have to stop crying.

VERONICA: I can't . . . I can't ever stop crying.

ISOBEL: I know! I know something to make you stop crying.
(Leaves)

VERONICA: *(Picks up photo of mama and puts it back on table)*
Mama . . . I'm sorry . . .
(Goes to screen. A great sense of loss) She didn't have to tear up
my souvenirs . . . I was saving them . . . I looked at them . . .
Every day . . . *(Gets down and goes through torn pieces)*

ISOBEL: *(Returns with old worn-out Raggedy Ann doll. Stops at doorway)* Look who's come to see you, Veronica. Miss Raggedy Ann.

VERONICA: *(Still going through scraps)* Yellowstone . . . Painted Desert . . .

ISOBEL: *(Approaching slowly. In mimicking voice)* "Veronica, please stop crying. I don't want to see you cry. It hurts my button eyes, because I can't cry along with you."

VERONICA: *(Rising slowly)* Raggedy Ann?

ISOBEL: She heard you crying. Way in the bedroom.

VERONICA: *(Takes doll, clutches her to her bosom tightly)* Raggedy Ann. My little Raggedy, Raggedy Ann. *(Sits in chair hugging doll)*

ISOBEL: That's much better. Much better. Raggedy Ann doesn't want Veronica crying anymore. She wants you to smile, like she is. And have a good time tonight.

VERONICA: I can't go. Not like this.

ISOBEL: Of course you can. Everything's all over now. Stand up, and I'll fix your sash. And you'll look as good as new.

VERONICA: *(Puts doll down. Stands listlessly)* I feel tired, Isobel . . . Old and tired—and empty inside.

ISOBEL: *(Backing off to survey. Then trying to inject new gaiety, claps her hands)* "Late, Late—You're going to be late!"

VERONICA: *(Like hearing a voice from the past)* Mama always said that—

ISOBEL: Right before every party—

VERONICA: *(In the past)* And, she'd be rushing around, looking for the present.

ISOBEL: "If you girls don't hurry, you'll be late for your own funeral!"

VERONICA: —The night of my ballet recital, I couldn't find my wings, and she started screaming at me—screaming and—

ISOBEL: *(Interrupting. Brightly clapping her hands in jump-rope fashion)*
"Late, Late—You're going to be late,
And being late is never great . . .
Late, Late—"

VERONICA: She was right, wasn't she—

ISOBEL: Who?

VERONICA: Mama . . . She was right wasn't she . . .

ISOBEL: Let's get our things together, so we're all ready when the taxi arrives. Put your fur on. Your hands feel all icy again.

VERONICA: Are you still making me go?

ISOBEL: It's too late to back out now.

VERONICA: I just don't feel—

ISOBEL: No more! You're going to be all right.

VERONICA: *(Stands stoically with wrap on)* I don't feel all right.

Horn toots. New Excitement takes over.

ISOBEL: Oh dear, the taxi already!

VERONICA: *(New panic)* I don't want to go, Isobel.

ISOBEL: There isn't time—not right now. *(Shoves gloves and purse in her hands)* Here. Now you have everything?

VERONICA: *(Pulled into the new frenzy)* I don't know. I think so.

ISOBEL: You better get going then.

VERONICA: *(Panicky)* My computer card! Where's my computer card?

ISOBEL: It was right here—

VERONICA: It has my number on. I don't remember what my number is.

ISOBEL: That card cost two hundred dollars! And now you've lost it.

VERONICA: I didn't lose it. It's here. Somewhere. *(They both go through things on table)*

ISOBEL: Always something you can't find at the last minute—

VERONICA: Here. Here it is.

ISOBEL: Put it in your purse! Now get going!

VERONICA: *(Stops still)* I feel sick again.

ISOBEL: *(Wheels her around)* There isn't time. That taxi's waiting—

VERONICA: *(Stops again)* I wish I'd never been born—

ISOBEL: *(Commanding)* Veronica!

VERONICA: I wish I hadn't been saved in mama and daddy's accident . . .

ISOBEL: You have to leave! *(Pushes her toward door)*

VERONICA: I'm going. You don't always have to push me.

ISOBEL: I'll wait up.

VERONICA: *(Turns back at doorway)* This is the last time you'll make me do anything! *(Exits. Door slams)*

ISOBEL: Goodbye. *(Goes to window, pulls back curtain. Waves silently. Turns off lights, so room is dimly lit. Turns and looks wearily at disarray)*
Gone . . . *(Picks up perfume bottle)* Everything . . . Nothing at all left from Miss Lilly. Except the music box.
(Sits and winds box) My present for my thirtieth birthday . . . Even that's wearing out. Music getting slower and slower, fainter and fainter. And one of these days, everything will be gone. Faded. Off in the distance. And I won't be able to bring

it back anymore . . . *(Up)* It's so empty in here. No one to talk
to. Veronica never goes anywhere without me.

(To Parrot) Admiral Bird, even you've run out of things to
say. Your time run out. Like the music box. Like all of us.
Everything slowing down . . .

*(Sits down. A feeling of emptiness prevails. Absently picks up Raggedy
Ann. Clutches doll to her)*

"Rockabye baby in the tree top—
When the wind blows the cradle will rock
When the bough breaks the cradle will fall—
And down will come

(Breaks into sobs) Mama—I've done everything I could. Now
there's nothing left to do.

*Rests head on table. Music box has stopped. She's fallen asleep. Lights
dim for a few moments.*

VERONICA *enters quietly, carrying her shoes. Bumps into chair.*

ISOBEL: *(Startled)* Veronica! When did you come home?

VERONICA: Just now—*(There sems to be a new vagueness about her)*

ISOBEL: I waited. But, I guess I was overtired.

VERONICA: That's all right.

ISOBEL: Did you come right home?

VERONICA: Yes.

ISOBEL: Didn't he take you anywhere?

VERONICA: Well, you see—

ISOBEL: *(Fully awake)* Sit down. Tell me all about it.

VERONICA: Couldn't we wait till tomorrow? I'm really quite
tired.

ISOBEL: I'm so anxious to hear—

VERONICA: *(Sits. Hesitates)* There's not much to tell—

ISOBEL: What did he look like? Did you like him?

VERONICA: Well, you see—I got there in time.

ISOBEL: I should hope so.

VERONICA: And, I was so frightened. I didn't want to go in. *(Stops)*

ISOBEL: Go on. Go on—

VERONICA: Computer Palace, it was like a huge barn. Not like a dance hall at all— There were printed signs all over—

ISOBEL: That's not important right now.

VERONICA: When you came in, they took your computer card and put it in a big machine that lit up and made all kinds of noises, and you were given a special number—

ISOBEL: Will you please get on to Arthur—

VERONICA: —And you waited in a special blocked off section, till your partner arrived.
And all night long, numbers were called, over the loudspeaker. Almost like bingo, with people jumping up when their number was called—

ISOBEL: Will you please tell me what happened when Arthur came!

VERONICA: *(Looking down)* He never came.

ISOBEL: What! He never showed up!

VERONICA: His number was never called.

ISOBEL: Are you sure you listened carefully. Weren't daydreaming as usual?

VERONICA: I listened, very closely. And they would repeat the number if no one came forward.

ISOBEL: I think that's terrible. I think you should get a refund. All that expense. Taxi. Wig. Wasted!

VERONICA: It wasn't wasted. *(Takes off fur)*

ISOBEL: I suppose you enjoyed sitting on the sidelines, as usual.

VERONICA: No, the waiting was awful.

ISOBEL: Let's go to bed. I'm so angry, I don't even feel like hot tea. And no wine for you tonight. You've had enough.

VERONICA: I don't want any.

ISOBEL: One night. Just one night, I wanted you to have a good time. Why, if I knew that Arthur's number, I'd call him this very minute. Well, we'll call Computor Suitor, first thing in the morning. Didn't you complain to anyone?

VERONICA: No, you see—

ISOBEL: Well, I certainly would have let someone know. They had his number. They could have called him.
How humiliating. To have to sit there all night, while the others danced. I didn't want you to be a wallflower. That's why I paid for this dance. One special night we planned for all these years—

VERONICA: But, I didn't sit all night—

ISOBEL: What?

VERONICA: I danced.

ISOBEL: With who? Did they find you a substitute? Well, we aren't paying for substitutes.

VERONICA: No, well, you see, I was sitting there, all nervous. And this gentleman, nearby—he was sitting and waiting too.

ISOBEL: You didn't talk to him, did you? Without an introduction—without knowing anything about him!

VERONICA: Not right away. But after awhile, he said, "Is that Paris Nights perfume you're wearing?"

ISOBEL: You are so naive about things.

VERONICA: I said "yes," and moved further away, so the perfume wouldn't bother him.

ISOBEL: You mean, so he wouldn't bother you.

VERONICA: Then he said, "That was my wife's favorite perfume—and you remind me of her."

ISOBEL: "You remind me of her—"—what an old line. I hope you didn't fall for it . . . But then you've never been out alone. Oh, I should have known . . .

VERONICA: He proceeded to ask me if my date had shown up. I said "No." He said his hadn't either, and that whether we matched or not, we should dance, not waste the whole evening.

ISOBEL: You didn't, did you!

VERONICA: *(Rises, looking out)* I don't know, Isobel. All of a sudden I was relaxed. I didn't know anything about him, and he didn't know anything about me. And I got up, and followed him. And there was this lovely waltz music, and they turned the lights low so you didn't even see the signs on the walls, only the crystal ball, shimmering like a huge bright star.

ISOBEL: So, you danced—with a perfect stranger.

VERONICA: Yes. I could do it, Isobel. It was like floating.

ISOBEL: I think we better retire. You can tell me the rest in the morning. You must be quite exhausted after all that dancing.

VERONICA: I don't feel tired. In fact, I feel like I'm still floating.

ISOBEL: I knew you shouldn't have taken that wine before you went—

(Flustered) Well, tomorrow—you'll feel different when things are back to normal. *(Puts things together on table)*

VERONICA: *(Quietly)* He asked to come and see me.

ISOBEL: *(Stops what she's doing)* What!

VERONICA: *(Not facing her)* He wanted to take me home. But, I said, "No."

ISOBEL: I should hope so.

VERONICA: I was so afraid, that once we left, everything would turn ugly, like in Cinderella.

ISOBEL: I don't know what's got into you tonight, Veronica, I don't know at all. Let's go to bed, and tomorrow—

VERONICA: He asked for my phone number, so he could call me.

ISOBEL: *(New alarm)* You didn't give it to him, did you? You couldn't have been so stupid as to give your phone number to a perfect stranger. Living alone on this empty road like we do.

VERONICA: I didn't know what to do.

ISOBEL: You really can't be trusted out alone, can you.

VERONICA: We had only practiced what to say to Arthur. This was so different. So, when he asked me for my phone number—

ISOBEL: You never give your phone number to a perfect stranger!
I've been thinking of having the phone disconnected anyway. No one calls here anymore. Just advertising. Needless expense. End of the month the phone goes! That's it! No more telephones in this house!

VERONICA: I didn't give him my number.

ISOBEL: At least you showed some sense.

VERONICA: But, he gave me his.

ISOBEL: What!

VERONICA: *(Gets card from her purse)* See. He wrote it on the back of my computer card. He said I should think it over. He didn't want to rush me. And, after I thought it over, to call him. Because, he really wanted to see me again.

ISOBEL: *(Snatches card from her)* This is all very ridiculous, you know. Picking up with a perfect stranger.

VERONICA: *(Taking card back)* He wasn't a stranger. He was a computer date.

ISOBEL: But, not yours! You knew nothing about him.

VERONICA: I liked it better not knowing whether he was a butcher or baker.

ISOBEL: Why didn't *his* date show up? Probably something wrong with him.

VERONICA: He told me all about himself.

ISOBEL: And you believed it?

VERONICA: Why not? We believed what Arthur said on his card.

ISOBEL: Those were true facts.

VERONICA: Were those true facts you put down on my card? You can put down anything on those cards.
But, when you sit next to a person, look them right in the eye, you know if they're telling the truth or not.

ISOBEL: Your mind is really clouded tonight. All this excitement has just been too much for you.
(Deliberately) I wouldn't be surprised if you made all this up. Just another one of your stories—

VERONICA: It's not a story. It really happened.

ISOBEL: You've always made up stories. Invented characters—

VERONICA: He wasn't made up. He was real.

ISOBEL: Veronica, I don't want to spoil all these nice new fantasies of yours, but, if you knew men like I do—all the things they will say, well, just to get you alone—for certain purposes.

VERONICA: He was a perfect gentleman!

ISOBEL: There! But, once he had you alone— Do you remember that movie I took you to, about this strange man, and this lonely lady—and what he did to her . . .

VERONICA: I don't care, Isobel! I liked him. I
really did. And, I'm going to bed now, and sleep on it, and
think about it.
You can't stop me from thinking about it. You never know
what goes on in my head.

ISOBEL: And sometimes you don't either.

VERONICA: —And if I still feel the same in the morning, I'm
going to call him.

ISOBEL: You're not going to call him!

VERONICA: *(A new strongness)* I'll decide about that in the
morning.

ISOBEL: You'll wake up tomorrow, and it'll all be like a far
away dream. Why, you won't remember if it happened or not.

VERONICA: I'll remember. The rest of my life . . .
(Picks up fur. Nonchalantly) I think I'll go to bed now. I'm really
quite tired.

ISOBEL: Yes, go to bed. You'll feel better—different, in the
morning. Just leave your things here.

VERONICA: *(Starts to leave, then goes to* ISOBEL*)* Thank you,
Isobel, for making me go. You always make me go places I
don't want to, and then I end up having such a good time.

ISOBEL: Yes, you do, don't you. *(Takes her hand and pats it)* You
see, I've always known what's best for you, haven't I.

VERONICA: Aren't you coming along?

ISOBEL: No, you just go ahead. use the bathroom first. I have
a few things to take care of here.

VERONICA: *(Just a bit of the old fright back)* Good night, Isobel.

ISOBEL: Good night, Veronica. Pleasant dreams.

VERONICA *leaves.* ISOBEL *straightens things up. Sees computer card
with phone number on it. Hesitates. Then walks over to parrot and*

tears it up into tiny pieces, letting them flutter to the floor like snow in front of the perch.

ISOBEL: *(Scolding)* Admiral Bird, did you get hungry and eat up Veronica's computer card with that man's phone number on it? That was naughty. That's wasn't a Polly cracker. That was one of Veronica's souvenirs.

(Walks awy) And now, she won't have any souvenirs left anymore. Nothing to save from tonight for her memory board . . .

(Sits wearing. Staring vacantly ahead)

(An inward cry) No souvenirs left at all . . . Nothing worth saving . . . Nothing . . . Nothing . . .

CURTAIN

PRODUCTION NOTES

TIME: Play runs about 35-40 minutes.

SETTING: No special setting or technical background is needed, only minimum furniture.

Minimum setting is table (folding card table), two chairs, genteel clutter.

Left is memory board, either a folding screen, or large piece of cardboard or wallboard, propped against chair.

Right is stand for Admiral Bird (either a floor lamp or folding clothes rack used for ironing).

ADMIRAL BIRD: Can be purchased plastic, or made of papier-mâché, with feathers glued on (From inexpensive father dusters that come in assorted colors). A coat hanger shaped into a circle forms the ring on which he perches.

BELLE OF THE BIJOU

Setting: Center Stage is a free standing screen covered with old movie memorabilia. Counter type table with phone and other items in front of it. Boxes of overflowing paraphernalia underneath. Nearer front, a high stool.

Scene opens: WOMAN *in her mid-sixties shuffles in Right, stopping outside Center area, defined by brighter lighting.*

She wears an old hat, shabby coat, galoshes and glasses. Carries an oversized purse and shopping bag.

Stops, looks about. Shiver runs through her.

CLARA BELLE: Like an icebox in here. Aagh, the dump always freezing anyway. Or like a furnace in summer.

"We ain't running no resort"—Jake's favorite phrase.

Tears imaginary poster off wall.

Get off the wall—you filthy!!

Tears it up and crumples it.

Garbage can. That's where you belong lady! Right in the garbage can—with all the rest of the trash around here . . .

"Didn't make no money—"

No wonder, kind of movies he showed. Even I couldn't watch them no more.

Years ago, I used to see every one. Some, maybe twenty times . . .

Aagh, who wants to come to this filthy neighborhood anymore, anyhow. Perverts. That's who. All that shows up. Sex store on the right. Go-go bar on the left.

About time I got outta here . . .

Sniffs.

Moldy. Whole place—moldy and rotting.

Huh, rest of those plaster birds will be dropping off the ceiling—one by one. Just like the time before, when they shut off the heat—during that war.

Well, I ain't gonna be around this time to watch them fall. Not me. I'll be in Hollywood. Where I shoulda gone in the first place.

Aagh, you get stuck working in one dumb place. Keep thinking things'll get better—they don't. Just keep getting worse and worse . . . And you just keep staying.

Well, now, I can finally go. Work for some big movie star. Live in one of their fancy houses.

Yeah, they'll be glad to hire me. Somebody what knows the business. Name any film. Who the stars were . . .

Runs hand along imaginary decorative wall carving.

Dirt! Everywhere—dirt!

Gold—those decorations used to be pure gold. Whole place used to be . . .

Walks to Stage Left.

Pity . . . Pity . . .

Tries wall switch.

Tightwad. Turned off the electricity too.

Takes flashlight from bag and shines it out.

Let's take one last look, Clara Belle. One last look at the beauty that used to be the Bijou.

Opens imaginary door and faces back.

Look what they did to this place . . .

That curtain—way back—shiny red velvet. Went up every night. Special show in itself. Now—dirty rotten rags.

Velvet seats. Now—purple plastic. Cut up. Peed on. Floor— gum, popcorn, schlobbered drinks— Place ain't fit for human.

Aagh, forget it. Forget it. Ain't your problem anymore.

Closes door and turns off flashlight.

Do what you came to do. Then get out fast as you can— like you shoulda done fifty years ago.

Gets keys from handbag.

Huh. Old geezer forgot to make me turn in my keys. So anxious to make his big announcement.

"Bijou's closing this Friday, Clara Belle. Tomorrow night's our last movie."

That's all he said. No, "Thank you"—not even a "Kiss my ass." Nothing.

All those years I put in here.

Well, whatta you expect from a doodlebum like him. Never did have a brain in that barrel. Anything for a buck. Anything . . .

"This is a business, Clara Belle, not the Salvation Army!"

Unlocking imaginary door. Once inside the lit circle, everything is real, because this is her real world. Looks about silently.

It's not the same . . .

Picks up phone.

Dead too . . .

(Into phone) "No, there ain't no movie tonight" . . . Ain't ever gonna be a movie in this place again.

Walks to window. Front.

Good-Man Hotel. How many years I looked out this window, seen that sign. Lights blinking on and off like a circus. Then Good Hotel— God Hotel— Now, nothing.

People still living there. Pensioners. Perverts. Never see them around. Sneak in and out.

Before—doormen, taxis. Always something going on over there. And the guests, come over here to the movies, every night. Running back after, dodging the cars. Happy people— on vacation—honeymoon . . .

I dunno. I always thought the Goodman would close down before we did.

Wonder what happened to Clarence—the doorman . . . He'd wave to me every night, minute my shade went up.

Shouting.

No! No movie! We're closed. See the sign! Closed!! For good!! Forever!

Bums. See somebody moving around in here, right away think we're open for business.

Go on, go find some other place to sleep.

Winos. Looking for a bed. That's all. Drunker wouldn't care if a movie was showing or not.

Takes off hat and coat. She's wearing button down sweater over old wool skirt.

Sooner I get started, sooner I get outta here. Don't know why I kept putting it off— Shoulda taken everything that last night— Wouldn't hadda come back at all.

Now, let's see. What to keep. What to throw away . . .

Picks up rolled up poster. Motherlike voice.

Good lord, Shirley— you still here yet? Why you ain't aged hardly none at all, have you.

Oh, those Saturday afternoons and Shirley Temple movies. Kids, lined up around the block. Special penny matinees. Some—could hardly reach the ticket window. Tips of curly heads, all you could see.

Haven't seen a kid in this place since . . .

Cute, she was so darn cute . . .

Stops. As if remembering. Takes off glasses. Fluffs hair.

"On a good ship Lollipop—"

Stops. Starts over.

"On a good ship Lollipop—"

Can't remember.

"It's a sweet trip— It's a sweet trip—
To the candy shop—and—and—"

Aagh, I used to know all the words. Every one.

How many times I see that picture. I had curls too. Blondie curls . . . Mama said I looked just like her, even if I was older . . . Mama put my hair up in rag curls every night . . .

Shakes her head as if she still had curls. Then runs fingers through her hair. Glasses back on. Crumples up poster.

Throw her away. No place today for bright eyes, dimpled cheeks . . . Blond curls . . .

Let's see what's in this box. Criminy—sheet music. Those things still here?

Blows off dust. Pages through several.

Nineteen twenty seven— Mama was playing piano here . . .

Sings.

"Tis the last rose of summer,
Left blooming alone . . . "

Bijou just opened. I was so excited— Mama playing the piano—silent movies. Me sitting in the front row, watching her and watching the magic screen.

Then mama got pleurisy so bad, couldn't play anymore, but could still work at the grocery store. They let me take over the piano here, not for long. Talkies came in, didn't need a piano player anymore. So they let me work the ticket box. Mikey and Rose were running the place . . . Wonderful couple . . .

Puts sheet music away.

I ain't played a piano—not since mama died. Well, had to sell the house. No room for a piano in the new flat. Landlady didn't like music anyways. Didn't like no activity at all. Mama and me, we'd sing and dance . . .

Wonder if they still got that old junker piano down in the basement here. Huh. Went down there and played, during those bad war movies. Didn't like watching them. Bombs. Killing. Then Jake, he says, "Cut out the piano playing. They can hear it upstairs!" Goof. All they could hear was bombs going off.

Ain't been down in that spooky basement since—Rats. Last one I saw down there was big enough for me. I says to Jake, "I'm not keeping anything down here anymore. Everything from my locker—going into my ticket booth."

"I ain't responsible, somebody steals your stuff," he says.

"You ain't responsible for nothing," I tell him. Aagh, you gotta tell him, or he'd walk all over you.

He'd be here every night. Just hanging around. Snooping.
See that the help didn't steal nothing, leave too early—or let
their friends sneak in.

Aagh, he probably made a good bundle. Bought the place
cheap enough during the Depression, from Mikey and Rose.
Squeezed out every penny—

Course, lately, business—bad . . . Awful . . .

You know, he had the eye for me too. Way back, before he
married. But, not my kind. Too rough. No education. Mama
didn't like him either . . .

Then, when his wife Emma died—he was down here the night
it happened—started shining around me real strong again—
till that young one, Gloria, came along.

Miss Gloria worked behind the candy counter. Didn't take
him long to take off after her and her red hair. She was green
around men. Didn't know him like I did.

Huh! Thought she was marrying some big movie tycoon. Sure
didn't last long. Took him for all she could. Then left him
for another Sugar Daddy.

I guess I didn't miss much, not getting married.

If you don't meet the right one, well— Not that I wasn't
without chances. Plenty of men stopped at this ticket window.

"Whatcha doing after the show tonight, honey?"

"That's personal," I'd say.

Oh, coupla times I was tempted. But, business and pleasure—
best not to mix.

Mama, she always kidded me about being in love with Clark
Gable. Just because I kept that big cardboard cutout of him
in my bedroom.

Well, Bijou was going to throw it out, so, I says to Jake, "Hey,
that's too nice a promo to throw out."

"You want it," he says, "take it."

Jake was pretty stingy too, about giving stuff away. But he
didn't like Clark, didn't like him at all.

Laughs.

Jake, he tried to grow a mustache—cookie duster, he called it. Never could. Made him so mad.

Well, Clark, he was just too big to fit in my ticket booth, so I take him home. Walk him all the way home that night—

And mama, she says she don't want no cardboard junk hanging around her living room. So I take him upstairs, to my bed-room.

You know, he really scared me, first coupla times I came home in the dark. Like a real man was standing there. Then, I just got used to him being there.

I gotta get him on the bus, somehow.

I can't leave him behind . . . Who would I say "Goodnight" to, and "Good morning" to? I always said it to mama. Then when she left—I had to talk to somebody—say goodnight to someone.

Takes glossy picture of Clark down from wall.

"Good night, Clark."

This one ain't as big, but it's still special . . .

Most special day of my life . . . Clark came to our town, promoting war bonds. Advertised he would give an autog-raphed picture to anyone who bought a five hundred dollar bond.

I borrowed the money. Well, it was to help out our country.

I can see it yet—plain as day. Band playing. Crowds all around. That platform, right in the center of downtown. Me—walking up—Him—giving me my war bond and his picture, smiling, saying real loud, "Thank you, honey," with that special twinkle in his eyes.

I think he was going to kiss me, but you know—with all those people watching.

I wanted to talk to him so bad. Tell him I seen "Gone With

the Wind" a hundred times. But I couldn't even open my mouth. Couldn't say nothing . . .

After, I wrote to him. When he went into the service. I mean, service men need letters from home. Keep up their morale.

Somehow, I always thought he'd answer me. Look in the mailbox first thing. Then, I'd worry maybe he was shot down . . .

I'd sneak out of my ticket box to watch the newsreels. Almost like being there. Everything so real. People getting shot apart. Houses blown up. Have to close my eyes. Then, they'd always show a short with Clark doing something special. So handsome in his uniform. Always smiling. Make me feel so proud, someone like him was defending our country.

Shame he had to die . . .

Wonderful thing about movies though, you kinda forget they're dead, because you keep seeing them live again and again in their pictures. And it's more like they're living than dead.

Takes romantic stance.

"I want you to faint . . . This is what you were meant for, Scarlet. None of the fools you've known have kissed you like this, have they . . . "

"Rhett—oh Rhett" . . .

Inward.

You're still alive to me, Clark. Still living . . .

Sits down, takes off galoshes.

I better get busy if I want get this junk cleared out . . . Oh, maybe a pill first. I dunno, since this place closed—can't sleep—can't eat. Doctor said these would help—only they make me feel funny, you know . . .

Takes pill.

Now, maybe everything won't be so mixed up.

Picks up roll of tickets. Lets them fall out.

Last roll of tickets.

Starts tearing them off, one at a time as she talks.

Three fifty sir, yes, that's the price of tickets today . . . . No, sir, I don't get rich on the profits, I only work here . . . . I don't know who gets the profits . . . Sir, the show starts in two minutes . . . . Sir, you only gave me a five dollar bill, *not* a ten dollar bill! . . .

No, I don't know what the film's about— Sir, I don't see the movies anymore . . . . I try not to even listen to them.

Turns Left.

Here, Jake. Here's the last ticket sold tonight. Last ticket sold ever . . . .

He counted those stubs like a miser, and blustered about if they didn't tally up at the end. He couldn't figure worth a damn anyway.

Always checking me out first. Usually was the ushers, pocketing tickets for their friends.

Every kid in town wanted to be an usher. Asking at the window all the time. Wear those fancy uniforms. Be the big man around the high school.

No more ushers. No more uniforms. No more nothing.

One by one they went. Jake became usher—ticket taker—candy seller. Later, he even closed down the candy counter, got a candy machine . . . . Oh, I missed the smell of popcorn . . . . Covered up those other smells.

Always threatening to get rid of the ticket seller too. Close up the box office, move it all inside—never did though.

Here, Jake, here's your whole damn roll of tickets—a lifetime admittance to the Bijou Theatre.

Those pills, getting to my head—so quick now . . .

Drapes tickets around her neck. Begins humming Hawaiian music.

"Aloha Oe— Aloha Oe—"

Giggles.

Dorothy Lamour and her sarong—

Does attempt at swaying. More languid.

Oh, I loved those pictures. All those strange foreign places— just like taking a trip . . .

Sways again. Runs hands along her body.

Hell, my figure was just as good as hers. Once, long time ago. Only nobody ever got to see it. Nobody. Wouldn't never let them. Later on, when it didn't matter so much, after mama was gone, and I wouldn't have to confess to nobody—nobody asked anymore . . . .

Jake, he'd keep hinting. Give anything for a peek. Even drilled a hole in the Ladies Room wall, so he could watch.

Didn't think I knew. I put gum over it all the time. Oh, he was a sneaky one. I never went to the bathroom, not while he was around. Lately, wouldn't even go near that place . . .

You know what he'd always say to me, "Come up and see me sometime!" He lived up on that hill . . . .

And you know what I'd always say . . .

Uses tickets as boa, Mae West stance.

"It's not the men in my life—it's the life in my men . . . "

Laughs.

And then—"Peel me a grape!"

God, she was gorgeous, that Mae West. More sex in that women, even with her clothes on.

And the men, pack them in. Nicely dressed ones too. Not the kind of bums you see come in here today.

I'd wear my hair like her, too. Blonde waves . . . . And the customers, the men, they'd kid me—"Hey Mae, come up and see me sometime . . . "

Mama even gave me a maribou wrap. Well, I put it on my Christmas list, kinda as a joke. Only reason I wore it down here was to keep warm.

"Mae's got her maribou on," they'd say.

Sings.

"A good man's hard to find . . . ."

Inward.

A good man's hard to find . . . .

I got tired of keeping my hair so blond—putting all those waves in . . .

Rolls tickets up slowly.

Admit one. Admit one—to what? The Wonders of the World.

As a barker.

Step right up, ladies and gentlemen—see "The Ten Commandments"! The bible come alive—the Red Sea parts—right before your eyes.

"Lost Horizon"!— Come and escape into your very own Shangri La—the world without any problems—

Escape—Escape—

"Mary Poppins"— "Peter Pan"—where people can fly—never grow up . . .

"Snow White," "Sleeping Beauty," "Fantasia"—where animals and flowers talk—and everyone lives happily after . . . .

Tears ticket in two, holds both parts up.

Admit One. Always one. Always alone . . . .

Oh sure, they'd come in by twos, on dates, all spruced up. The young guy, hair slicked back, importantly he'd hand me a fiver. And the girl, tipsy on her wobbly heels, smelling of Blue Waltz perfume—always smiling. They'd head right for the balcony. "Necker's Heaven."

Balcony? Closed down now. What went on up there—after—wasn't necking. Well, what did he expect, kind of movies he put on.

To ticket window.

No sonny, you ain't getting in, you ain't eighteen and I ain't letting you in to see this show—I don't care if he is your father . . . .

Picks up phone.

No sir, it's an adult movie. Yes sir, it's x-rated. no sir, I can't tell you what it's about . . .

I don't care Jake, I'm not letting no young boy in to see this filth! You want the law on you. You want this place closed down! They put you in jail—who's gonna run the show then!

Me, I can always find another job.

Back to boxes.

I'll never get this place cleaned up . . . .

Opens old suitcase.

Mama's things. I even forgot they were here. That's right, I didn't want the landlady snooping through them, trying them on.

I only kept these special things. Everything else went—

Mama's hat. Oh, she looked so pretty in it—just like Jeanette McDonald.

Puts on soft picture hat.

"I am calling you—oo-oo-oo—
Say you love me too-oo-oo—"

Hums a bit.

She was some star! People came out from her movies, humming those tunes . . .

Her and Nelson. Perfect pair.

Sings.

"Sweetheart, sweetheart, sweetheart—"

Dances a bit.

"Do you remember the day— When we were so happy and gay—"

Pauses, takes hat off.

Nobody wears hats anymore . . .

Maybe down south they still do.

Holds hat in hand, pensively.

"Ah don't want realism—ah want magic . . . Yes, yes, magic!
I try to give that to people . . . . Ah don't tell truth, ah tell
what ought to be truth— Don't turn the light on!"

Covers face. Retains southern accent.

Such a sad picture—that "Streetcar." At the end, when they
hauled Blanche off . . . Sad . . .

That Vivien Leigh—how an English girl could play those
Southern belles.

"Oh Rhett, ah was so cold and hungry and tired! And I
couldn't find it! I ran and ran and I couldn't find it! . . . I
don't know! I've always dreamed that dream and I never
know! I just run and run and hunt and can't ever find what
I'm hunting for! I know I'd be safe forever if I could find it!"

Find it—we never find it . . .

*Pause. Rummages through suitcase. Holds up long chiffon gown in
front of her.*

Mama looked just like Ginger Rogers in this dress. Only she
always said, "I can't look like Ginger Rogers, unless I have a
Fred Astaire—" And papa, wherever he was—he was no Fred
Astaire. Wallace Beery, that's more who he looked like—his
picture. I never saw him. Don't remember him at all . . .

Sings and dances a bit.

"Dancing in the Dark . . . "

Hums.

I'll keep this too. Might need such a dress, in California—for those fancy parties.

Picks up red patent high-heeled shoes.

Good lord, that's where they are. The red shoes of the Good Witch of the North . . . . I'd dress up in them—pretend—wave a magic wand . . . .

Sings.

"Somewhere over the Rainbow—"

That was a beautiful movie.

"We're off to see the Wizard—
The wonderful Wizard of Oz–"

Poor Judy—Dorothy, all she wanted was to go home again.

I would of stayed in Emerald City. Best part of the movie. Everything turned green. The tiny Munchkins—

But Dorothy, she just wanted to go home.

"Auntie Em—Auntie Em—Toto, where are you?"

And she wakes up in her own bed. Was all a dream. A big big dream. All those places she'd been to, wonderful things she'd seen—they weren't real at all. Only a dream . . .

Movies are like that—like dreaming and when they're over, it's like waking up.

Why do I keep thinking of all that stuff.

Maybe a cup of coffee would help right now.

Finds cup.

Forgot. No electricity. No hot water.

Last of the Dish Night cups.

Leftover. Zasu Pitts. Nobody wanted that cup much.

I wanted the whole set. New star each week. But Jake, he wouldn't give one away, not without a ticket. So I bought tickets for—Norma Shearer—Irene Dunne—Carole Lombard—Clark's wife . . .

Broke them all, carrying them home one night. Icy. I put my hand out. Didn't help none. Broke them all. My arm too. Hurt so. I sat there crying—mostly about those broken cups. Arm in a cast for months, I still came to work. Never missed a day—except those weeks after mama died.

Zasu's all that's left. Everybody wants the pretty ones.

Dish Night. Bank Night. Bingo. Anything to bring the money in. Tough days, those were.

Amateur contests too. Sometimes, when the piano player didn't show up, Jake, he'd rush in here, "Clara Belle, quick, go on, get out there, play the piano! I'll sell the tickets."

Make me so mad. He always messed this office up so.

Friday night serials . . . Flash Gordon . . . Charlie Chan . . . Tom Mix . . . .

And cartoons. All day Saturday. All day Sunday. Nobody used baby sitters those days. Just sent the kids to the movies.

And Jake, he'd bring those crying kids in here. Some days, this ticket office would be jammed up with them.

Parents forget to pick them up. Not too many had phones those days . . .

I even had to walk some home. Half didn't know where they lived. So small, could hardly talk. Then, we had to call the police. Hated to do that. Not Jake.

Right away, "Call the police. Call the police. Once the movie's over, I ain't responsible for them anymore . . . . People wanta have kids, they should take care of them!"

Used to bother him to hear the kids laugh too.

"Hyenas, that's what they sound like. A bunch of laughing hyenas."

Kids jiggered Jake up so—he stopped having those comedy shows.

"No money in them," he says, "no money—only trouble."

Betty Boop. Felix the Cat. Popeye . . . . All those good cartoons, one right after another. Kids running up and down the aisles. Losing their money, their mittens—their baby sister.

"Miss Belle, I can't find Bitsy anywhere . . . ." "Miss Belle, my brother has to go to the bafroom, can he come in the Ladies Room with me? . . . " "Miss Belle, I like you . . . ."

I would have liked to have had kids . . .

Chilly in here . . .

Finds fur piece and drapes around her neck.

Mama's fur . . .

Rubs hands together.

Winter time always like ice in here. Me, wearing mama's fur.

Feel just like I was in "Dr. Zhivago." Snow falling outside. Forget I was even in here . . . .

Hums "Somewhere My Love."

Him—sitting in his ice palace. Writing his love poems. Gloves on his hands. Frost on his mouth.

Then, going through all that snow, just to find his true love again. Always searching, a whole lifetime, just for a glimpse of her. And at the end, they go past each other, without even knowing . . . .

Does each person only have one true love . . . And what if you never meet that other person . . .

Pulls fur tighter. Hums again.

Omar Shariff, he sure was handsome. But not like Clark. There never was no one like Clark.

"Frankly, my dear, I don't give a damn!"

Picks up cup again. Looks down into it, as if into a well.

"I'm wishing (echo) I'm wishing—
For the one I love (echo) For the one I love—
To find me— To find me—
Today— Today— Today . . . ."

Snow White. Such a beautiful girl—and that scarey witch—

"Come little girl—a nice bite of the apple."

"Don't eat it!" the kids screaming. Me too sometimes.

Then those dwarfs crying around her glass casket. Her waiting for Prince Charming, to wake her up, with the kiss of love.

How many times I sat through that picture—Always waiting for that happy ending, like I didn't know what was going to happen.

Sings.

"Heigh ho, Heigh ho— It's off to work we go—"

Let's see, there was Dopey—Sneezy—Grumpy—and—and—

Sings.

"Just whistle while you work—"

Attempts to whistle.

Yeah, I better get back to work here too. Pretty soon that daylight's gonna be gone. Whole place will be dark.

You know, inside that theater there, daylight never got in. Sixty years and never one speck of sunlight. Like it wasn't part of the outside world at all.

Come on, Clara Belle, come on.

Picks up stack of magazines.

Movie magazines—used to buy every one.

Paging.

Great Garbo— Don't come like her anymore . . .

Dramatic pose.

Her—dying in "Camille." I cried every time. Sometimes, coupla times a night.

Norma Shearer. Myrna Loy. Claudette—whatever happened to them. Rich. Famous. Then what? What do you have after that?

Ann Miller and her taps—Eleanor Powell.

Does a few taps.

Always wanted to—but never could get that dance right.

Charlie Chaplin, him I could do—

Does Charlie Chaplin walk. Laughs.

He was so funny—till he started talking.

Marx Brothers. Ritz Brothers. Place inside shaking with laughs.

You don't hear them laughing in there—not anymore. X-movies aren't funny . . .

Don't sit together either. Big spaces between them.

Throw them out. Stacks more at home. Too heavy to take to California. Besides, out there, I'll be seeing the real thing.

Wonder whose house I'll be living in . . . . That's how I'll pick who I work for—ask who lived in the house before.

Maybe Rudolph Valentino, or John Gilbert, or—I wouldn't want to live in Clark's house. I don't know—I'd just feel—funny . . .

Clippings—clippings—

Lets them flutter like ticker tape.

I'd sit here reading and clipping. Anything about movie stars . . . . I knew every Academy Award—

Once I got my TV, I'd take off Academy Award night. Jake, he didn't like it, but the place was dead anyway.

Best thing I did, buy that television. Just like being there, Academy Award night, seeing all the stars, close up—almost touch them.

TV has those old movies too. I can lock up here and go home and watch the old movies. Better than the ones here.

Asked Jake if I could bring a portable in the booth.

"Nothing doing," he says. "We're here to make money, not be entertained . . . ."

Set ain't working too good lately. Not taking it along. Besides, those fancy Hollywood houses all have TV. One in every room. Big ones too. Color. Some of those houses even have their own movie room . . . . That would be something!

Goes thorugh clips, throwing out as she talks.

Spencer Tracy dies—Bing Crosby dies—Vivien Leigh—they all go, sooner or later.

All stories on their deaths. None on their births. Well, when you're born, who knows if you're going to be famous or not.

Divorces . . . Marriages . . . Sometimes hard to keep track who was married to who.

Throw them all out. I ain't never going to put them in a scrapbook. Not anymore. Always thought I would. But I couldn't keep up—never even get enough ahead—with any-thing . . . .

Come on, Clara Belle, come on.

Picks up still photo.

Quasidmodo . . . Now, what did I keep that picture for. Hunch Back of Notre Dame. Ugly!

Every one of them was ugly—Charles Laughton—Lon Chaney—

You couldn't help feeling sorry for that creature though. Loving Esmerelda like he did. Knowing it was no use—she'd never love him back. Didn't matter to him. Some loves are like that.

And him walking around that wheel. Bleeding. Thirsty.

Does Hunchback stance, tongue hanging sideways.

"Watah! Watah!"

I wanted to give him water so bad . . .

How that guy could live up there in that little belfry, not any bigger than this place, away from everybody.

Deaf too. Deaf to everything but his own little world. Only hearing those bells. His only bright spot—loving Esmeralda.

Maybe I'll keep him. Kept him all those years . . . .

Pulls string on back wall. Feebly mimicking a call.

Help . . . . Help . . . .

Laughs.

My call for help. What a laugh.

I risked my life to save his damn money.

First time the robbers came—right up to my box office window, I said, "You'll have to come in here to get it." Then ducked down, quick as a blink.

"They could of shot you!" Jake yells after. I didn't care. Was right after mama died, and I didn't care about much . . .

Few years later, creeps came again. So, I did the same thing.

Jake, he yells, "I ain't risking losing my money anymore." So he puts in this dingaling string.

"You just pull this rope, Clara Belle, and a bell rings in the projection booth."

Big laugh. Heinie, in the projector booth, he was always half dead anyway. Like Quaismodo up there in his belfry. What would a poop like him do anyhow if I was being robbed?

Anyways, no more robbers came. I was waiting for them, cause next time I was gonna give them the whole damn cash box.

But you wait for something, it never happens. "Watched pot, never boils," mama would say.

Picks up picture in frame.

Mama . . . . I don't now why I kept you down here. With all the celebrities.

Well, she kinda liked the stars too. Named me after Clara Bow. Only, she called me Clara Belle, so she wouldn't mix us up.

Jake, he always called me Miss Boginski—at first. Then, "Ding Dong Belle"—thought that was funny. I never did.

Then Clara Belle—or just Miss Belle. —"Miss Belle of the Bijou" he'd say. Well, this always was my place . . . . Belle of the Bijou—

Picks up keys.

Wonder if he wants his keys back.

Place could open up again. Maybe times will change. People will get tired of seeing only sex and crime. They'll want pretty movies again . . . .

Nah, they got television.

Throws down keys. Sits.

But television's not the same. Everything squashed down into that dinky box. Stars should be on great big screens—bigger than life. With voices coming from all around, like you were right in the middle, part of the whole thing. That's how being at a movie is.

And even in the dark, you're not alone. Always people there somewhere, watching with you. Laughing, crying. And even if you sit alone, you really aren't.

At home, watching TV, you laugh and cry all by yourself. It's not the same . . .

Up.

Nah, they'll never open this place up again . . .

Closing them up all over town. Except the shopping centers.

Went to one of them once. Never again. Like a hallway. Long, narrow. Concrete walls. Skimpy screen. No fancy decorations even. Nothing!

Movie theaters have got to be special places. That's how they used to build them. Going there, was an event. Gone . . . . One by one they're going . . . And nobody's trying to save them . . .

If I had money, I'd open my own theater. Run all the beautiful shows, over and over. "Belle's Beautiful Bijou"—

Who'd come? Who'd come anymore . . .

Looks as if she's going to cry. Takes a pill.

I better take another pill. I sure don't want to get feeling funny again . . . . Not before my trip.

This time, I knew it was coming—week after the theater shut down, I began feeling just like after mama died.

So I went to the doctor right away. He gave me these pills. And he said, anytime I feel a bad spell coming on—

Well, out in California, I won't need any pills. All that fresh air, sunshine. Oranges right off the trees.

Takes calendar off wall.

Throw this out too. What day it is—doesn't matter here anymore.

Flips pages.

The old movies—pages would flip off the calendars—to show time going by.

Leaves would fall and seasons pass . . . . And in one short hour you could see a whole lifetime of a person. See them young. See them old.

"Wuthering Heights" that was my favorite growing up picture. That handsome Heathcliff—always loving Cathy. Even when he was just a stableboy.

And Merle Oberon growing up, beautiful and sassy. And then there's this tragedy and Heathcliff is dead— Her great true love, gone. And she wanders those misty moors calling out to him . . . "Heathcliff—Heathcliff." Went right through me . . .

And even though he was dead, he came back. His whole spirit was able to come back, because of their great love.

Sometimes, I feel like Clark can do that—as if his spirit were floating around his cardboard figure.

I guess in movies that's okay to happen. But in real life, you tell somebody that, they put you in a looney bin for sure. I'd never tell anybody what goes on between Clark and me . . . Nobody . . .

Picks up sign.

"Coming Attractions . . . " There ain't no more coming attractions. Nothing coming at all. Everything's happened already.

"Past Attractions"—"Come and see the Past Attractions."

Throws sign in basket.

Mama always said, everything changes in life. All your dreams, your hopes—they never turn out like you think.

Except in movies. There, everything stays the same. People never grow old. End never changes.

Sits.

What if there were movie reels wound up inside our head and our life just plays out till the film is used up, and then it's over. And there's nobody there to rewind and play it again.

If there were reels inside our heads—then everything's set beforehand—and you couldn't make any changes, even if you wanted to. You couldn't make a different ending at all. It's all set beforehand. You get to the end of the reel—that's it. Everything's over.

Nah, there ain't no screen in there to show your life on. What kinda crazy ideas am I thinking.

Who'd wanta see my life anyway . . .

Who'd wanta play it all over again . . .

Somedays it is like moving pictures were going on in my head. I keep seeing parts of certain movies over and over—like soldiers, parts of the war flashes back at them. Sometimes, the movies in my head mix up together and I can't straighten them out—which part belongs to which movie. Even when I sleep, they begin showing over again . . .

Getting warm in here. Head feels funny too. Must be those pills.

Packs Mama's clothes into shopping bag as she talks.

Gotta make sure to fix me something to eat when I get home. Last time I took those pills, I forgot all about eating. Well, when you live alone, nobody to sit down to a meal with. You could sleep all day and nobody would wake you up—nobody . . .

I shoulda had a dog. After mama died, and after that last Lassie picture, I was gonna buy me a big fluffy dog.

"Woof—woof—I'm glad to see you!"

But then, the landlady—well, I didn't even ask her.

If I did have a dog, then now, I'd only have to worry what to do with it. That's the trouble, you get attached to something— animals, places—people— Painful when they go away . . . .

Puts galoshes and coat on.

Take this bag of junk and get outta here. They can burn the whole place down now, for all I care.

Tears off what's left on the back wall, almost viciously.

Everything goes! Everything including me! Yeah, after all these years I'm finally getting out! Finally! And I'm not sorry one bit!

Picks up phone.

Hello—Jake—it's all cleaned out. Yeah, I took what I wanted. You can throw away the rest. No, I didn't take nothing what doesn't belong to me . . . I know I ain't got another check coming. I ain't got nothing coming anymore . . .

Yeah, I'll send you a postcard—

Puts phone down.

How can I send you a card, Jake. I don't even know where you live . . .

Jake DePalma—Top of the Hill—Overlooking the Bijou Theatre.

All those years—and I never knew his address.

Really getting dark now.

Wouldn't you know, here comes another one of them. They're never going to let me alone.

Go on—get outta here! No show tonight! Never going to be another show in this place again!

You'll never see me here again either. I'm getting out. Right now! And never coming back!!

Realization. Tears forming.

Never coming back . . .

Looks around, bewildered.

This place is all I've known. All I've ever done . . .

What am I going to do?

Where am I going to go?

I'm too old to start over again. Too worn out to go half way across the country . . .

I don't know anybody out in California. I'd probably get lost, wouldn't know who to ask . . .

Who'd give me a job anyway. All I know is how to sell tickets.

Who's going to help me?

Sobs.

I can't leave here. I got nowhere's to go . . .

Pulls string. An inner cry.

Help . . . Help . . .

Another yank that pulls string down. A loud cry.

Help!!

Softer.

Help . . . help . . . help . . .

Holding onto broken string.

There's no one to hear me.
They're gone . . . Everybody . . .
Jake . . .
Mama . . .
Clark . . .
Clark, no he isn't gone, he's still alive, still living in all those old movies.
And he's still my my bedroom, saying "Good morning Clara Belle," "Good night Clara Belle . . . "

As if she's transformed into Scarlet. Stands in spotlight.

"Ah cain't let him go! Ah cain't! Ah won't think about losing him now! Ah'll go crazy if ah do! . . . Ah'll think about it tomorrow . . . "

Back as herself.

Tomorrow . . . I've got to go to California. I promised Clark I'd take him with me. Visit his grave. Walk in his footprints at the Chinese Theatre . . .

Turns back as Scarlet.

"As God is my witness . . . As God is my witness . . . They're not going to lick me! . . . I'm going to live through this and when it's over—I'll never be hungry again . . . "

Back as herself.

Tomorrow—tomorrow, I'm going to go buy that bus ticket.

Picks up her bag and starts walking off. Stops. Takes one last look. With a special radiancy.

"After all, tomorrow is another day . . . "

Turns and slowly walks off as lights dim.

CURTAIN

BATTERY

BY DANIEL THERRIAULT

Electricity is the central metaphor and an expressive image for this unusual love story set in an electrical workshop.